The Disney BOOK

A Celebration of the Worlds of Disney

NEW EDITION

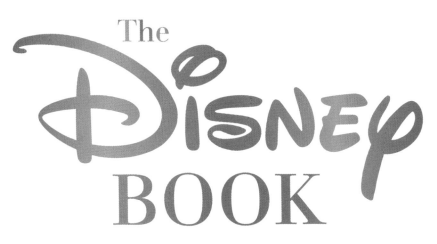

The Disney BOOK

A Celebration of the Worlds of Disney

NEW EDITION

Written by Jim Fanning and Tracey Miller-Zarneke

Contents

▲ See p. 71

▲ See p. 26

▲ See p. 57

▲ See p. 44

▲ See p. 82

▲ See p. 94

▲ See p. 117

▲ See p. 143

▶ See p. 75

▶ See p. 149

▲ See
p. 150

▲ See
p. 179

▲ See p. 202

▲ See p. 251

◀ See p. 196

▶ See p. 192

Introduction

Disney means enchantment, fun, and adventure—but beyond that, a touching of the heart, an aspirational stirring of the soul, a feeling of belonging. Behind all the emotion and artistry is a special type of imagination; a creativity born of artists and animators, actors and directors, Imagineers and Cast Members. It is an artistry evident not only in a completed film or a theme park but also in the paintings, drawings, and other artworks produced by the Disney artisans. All of this and more makes up *The Disney Book*.

From the start, Walt wanted the name Disney to represent quality, a novel entertainment that was uniquely engaging. And for more than 90 years, Walt and those who carry on his creative heritage have made that name symbolize a magic that transcends mere entertainment.

This book covers many of the highlights of this singular history. Since its own history is unusually important to the never-ending evolution of Disney, that history is every bit as fascinating as the productions, programs, and parks themselves. And as that history has long held a remarkable fascination for Disney fans of every age and ilk, we are very happy to bring together this tome of Disney treasures for you.

Most images in *The Disney Book* were selected from the jam-packed vaults of The Walt Disney Company. With more than 9,000 boxes of documents and merchandise items, as well as several thousand historic props and costume pieces—from the earliest Mickey Mouse Club to the latest *Pirates of the Caribbean* film—the Walt Disney Archives documents Disney history as it happens. The Walt Disney Archives Photo Library houses more than four million images. The various types of negatives and color transparencies preserved in the Archives cover all aspects of Disney history, from its beginnings to the present. From concept art to the final film frames, the Walt Disney Animation Research Library houses more than 65 million pieces of original artwork that helped create the beloved Disney films, both classic and contemporary. And from Walt Disney Imagineering, the Slide Library provided select photos of Imagineers and their creations while the Art Library offered a rich tapestry of theme-park masterpieces.

As you can see from the treasures in this book, this wonderful world, as Disney is often described, is actually a vast universe. From Mickey Mouse to Baymax, from *Cinderella* to *Frozen*, and the global theme park kingdom on which the sun never sets, Disney is an ever-expanding, always enchanting subject. This book gives you a glimpse into the magic that made "the Mouse"—and all that he represents.

By Jim Fanning
(First edition, 2015)

The Disney Book is a classic collective peek at now more than a century's worth of art and creativity that has sprung from a deep well of inspiration—Walt Disney. Whether it's conveyed through screened entertainment (be it animation or live-action, musicals or documentaries); or through theme park, theater, gaming, and travel experiences; or through collectibles large and small, the imaginative Disney spirit has brought joy and heartwarming memories to generations of audiences, tourists, and collectors alike.

As entertainment and experiences have widened, so too has Disney's pool of historic resources. In addition to the tens of millions of physical objects housed in its collection, the Walt Disney Animation Research Library now has access to millions of born-digital artworks from the ever-expanding slate of recent animated films.

While the world of Disney has come to incorporate many creative partnerships over the years—adding richness to the cast of characters, and breadth to the universe once their realms were brought into the Disney fold—the focus of The Disney Book mostly remains on those characters and concepts that were initially developed within the central Disney brain trust.

I hope you enjoy the magic of Disney, old and new and ever-evolving, within the pages of The Disney Book.

Lovingly updated with gratitude for the past and excitement for the future ...

By Tracey Miller-Zarneke
(Updated edition, 2023)

1920s and 1930s

When Walt Disney founded his studio in 1923, black-and-white silent films were state-of-the-art and animated shorts were mere fillers. By the end of the 1930s, Disney led the way in sound and color and transformed the lowly cartoon into an art form. Along the way, Walt and his artists developed a special style of storytelling, a way of creating unforgettable characters, and principles of entertainment that the company Walt founded still follows today.

This timeline paints a broad stroke highlighting some of the releases Disney has shared with the world each year.

1924

Alice Comedies: ●····
Alice's Spooky Adventure

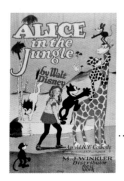

1925

Alice Comedies: ●····
Alice in the Jungle

1926

Alice Comedies: ●····
Alice's Spanish Guitar

1927

Oswald the Lucky Rabbit: ●····
Trolley Troubles

1932

Silly Symphony: ● ★····
Flowers and Trees

1933

Silly Symphony: ● ★····
Three Little Pigs

1934

Silly Symphony: ●····
The Wise Little Hen

1935

Mickey Mouse: ●····
The Band Concert

1920

Walt working at a newspaper
in Kansas City

1921

Newman Theater's
first Laugh-O-gram

1922

Jack and the Beanstalk
Laugh-O-gram

1923

Alice's Wonderland

Disney Brothers
Cartoon Studio formed

1928

Mickey Mouse: *Steamboat Willie*

1929

Silly Symphony:
The Skeleton Dance

1930

Mickey Mouse: *The Fire Fighters*

1931

Silly Symphony:
The Ugly Duckling

1936

Mickey Mouse:
Thru the Mirror

1937

*Snow White and the
Seven Dwarfs* (initial release)

1938

Silly Symphony:
Merbabies

1939

Donald Duck:
The Autograph Hound

1940s and 1950s

KEY
- ☙ Important events
- ○ Documentary
- ● Nature documentary
- ● Hand-drawn animated
- ● Live-action
- ○ CG animation
- ● Live-action/Animated hybrid
- ● Stop-motion
- ★ Academy Award® winner

Dates refer to year of U.S. general release

During World War II, Walt educated and inspired Allied forces by contributing to military training films and morale-boosting cinematic explorations. He was also continually developing new filmmaking techniques. In the 1950s, after embracing the technology of television, Walt created an entirely new form of entertainment—the theme park—in the form of a magic kingdom known as Disneyland Park.

1944
First Aiders ●····

1945
The Three Caballeros ●
Roy O. Disney becomes president ☙
of Walt Disney Productions

1946
Make Mine Music ●

1947
Fun and Fancy Free ●····

1952
The Story of Robin Hood ●····
and His Merrie Men

1953
Peter Pan ●····
The Sword and the Rose ●
The Living Desert ● ★

1954
Rob Roy, the Highland Rogue ●
The Vanishing Prairie ● ★
20,000 Leagues Under the Sea ● ★····

1955
Disneyland opens ☙····
Davy Crockett, ●
King of the Wild Frontier
Lady and the Tramp ●
The African Lion ○
Mickey Mouse Club ●
The Littlest Outlaw ●

1940

Pinocchio ● ★···
Fantasia ●

1941

The Reluctant Dragon ●
Dumbo ● ★···

1942

Bambi ●····

1943

Saludos Amigos ●
Victory Through Air Power ●

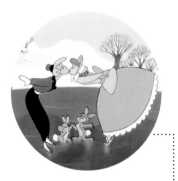

1948

Melody Time ●····
Seal Island (initial release) ●

1949

So Dear to My Heart ●
*The Adventures of Ichabod
and Mr. Toad* ●

1950

Cinderella ●····
Treasure Island ●

1951

Alice in Wonderland ●····

1956

The Great Locomotive Chase ●····
Davy Crockett and the River Pirates ●
(theatrical release)
Secrets of Life ●

1957

Johnny Tremain ●
Perri ●
Old Yeller ●····

1958

The Light in the Forest ●
White Wilderness ● ★···
Tonka ●

1959

Sleeping Beauty ●····
The Shaggy Dog ●
Darby O'Gill and the Little People ●
Third Man on the Mountain ●

1960s and 1970s

Walt innovated again with a global live audience at the 1964–1965 New York World's Fair, new theme park adventures and plans, and a blockbuster musical about a magical nanny. Five years after Walt's death in 1966, the new Walt Disney World project in Florida opened. This set the stage for a constantly evolving expression of the Imagineering art form. Disney kept Walt's imaginative spirit alive with a series of animated features, each more popular than the one before.

1964

The Misadventures of Merlin Jones ●
A Tiger Walks ●
The Moon-Spinners ●
Mary Poppins ● ★
Emil and the Detectives ●
Those Calloways ●

1965

The Monkey's Uncle ●
That Darn Cat! ●

1966

The Ugly Dachshund ●
Lt. Robin Crusoe, U.S.N. ●
The Fighting Prince of Donegal ●
Follow Me, Boys! ●
Walt Disney dies 🐭

1967

Monkeys, Go Home! ●
The Adventures of Bullwhip Griffin ●
The Happiest Millionaire ●
The Gnome-Mobile ●
The Jungle Book ●
Charlie, The Lonesome Cougar ●

1972

The Biscuit Eater ●
Napoleon and Samantha ●
Now You See Him, ●
Now You Don't
Run, Cougar, Run ●
Snowball Express ●

1973

The World's Greatest Athlete ●
Charley and the Angel ●
One Little Indian ●
Robin Hood ●
Superdad ●

1974

The Bears and I ●
The Castaway Cowboy ●
The Island at the Top of the World ●

1975

The Strongest Man in the World ●
Escape to Witch Mountain ●
The Apple Dumpling Gang ●
One of Our Dinosaurs Is Missing ●
Ride A Wild Pony ●

1960

Toby Tyler, or Ten Weeks with a Circus ●
Kidnapped ●
Pollyanna ●
The Sign of Zorro ●
Jungle Cat ●
Ten Who Dared ●
Swiss Family Robinson ●
The Horse With the Flying Tail ● ★

1961

One Hundred and One Dalmatians ● ⋯
The Absent-Minded Professor ●
The Parent Trap ●
Nikki: Wild Dog of the North ●
Greyfriars Bobby ●
Babes in Toyland ●

1962

Moon Pilot ●
Bon Voyage ●
Big Red ●
Almost Angels ●
The Legend of Lobo ●
In Search of the Castaways ●

1963

Son of Flubber ●
Miracle of the White Stallions ●
Savage Sam ●
Summer Magic ●
The Sword in the Stone ● ⋯
The Three Lives of Thomasina ●

1968

Blackbeard's Ghost ●
The One and Only, Genuine, ●
Original Family Band
Never a Dull Moment ●
The Horse in the Gray Flannel Suit ●

1969

Smith! ●
Rascal ●
The Computer Wore Tennis Shoes ● ⋯

1970

King of the Grizzlies ●
The Boatniks ●
The Aristocats ● ⋯

1971

Walt Disney World Resort opens ➥ ⋯
The Wild Country ●
The Barefoot Executive ●
Scandalous John ●
The Million Dollar Duck ●
Bedknobs and Broomsticks ● ★

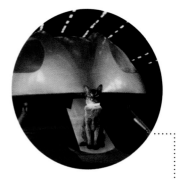

1976

No Deposit, No Return ●
Gus ●
Treasure of Matecumbe ●
The Shaggy D.A. ● ⋯

1977

"New" Mickey Mouse Club ●
Freaky Friday ●
The Littlest Horse Thieves ●
The Many Adventures
of Winnie the Pooh
The Rescuers ●
Pete's Dragon ● ⋯
Candleshoe ●

1978

Return from Witch Mountain ●
The Cat From Outer Space ● ⋯
Hot Lead and Cold Feet ●

1979

The North Avenue Irregulars ●
The Apple Dumpling ●
Gang Rides Again
Unidentified Flying Oddball ●
The Black Hole ● ⋯

1980s and 1990s

With Tokyo Disneyland, the first Disney theme park outside the U.S., Disney widened its kingdom across the globe. Dynamic new leadership revitalized traditions and challenged creative and business growth, resulting in such expansions as the acquisition of the ABC television network, as well as a re-flowering of the art form Walt created, the hand-drawn animated feature. The company celebrated the launch of the Disney Cruise Line on the seas and the revolutionary evolution of computer-animated films on screens.

1984

Touchstone Pictures 🐭
is established
Frankenweenie (featurette) ●

1985

Return to Oz ●
The Black Cauldron ●
The Journey of Natty Gann ●
One Magic Christmas ●

1986

The Great Mouse Detective ●
Flight of the Navigator ●

1987

Benji the Hunted ●
DuckTales ●

1992

Newsies ●
Euro Disney Resort 🐭
(now Disneyland Paris)
opens near Paris, France
Honey, I Blew Up the Kid ●
The Mighty Ducks ●
Aladdin ● ★
The Muppet Christmas Carol ●

1993

Homeward Bound: ●
The Incredible Journey
A Far Off Place ●
The Adventures of Huck Finn ●
Hocus Pocus ●
Cool Runnings ●
Tim Burton's *The Nightmare* ●
Before Christmas
The Three Musketeers ●

1994

Disney Interactive is founded 🐭
Iron Will ●
Blank Check ●
D2: The Mighty Ducks ●
White Fang 2: Myth of the White Wolf ●
The Lion King ● ★
Angels in the Outfield ●
Squanto: A Warrior's Tale ●
The Santa Clause ●
Rudyard Kipling's The Jungle Book ●

1995

Heavyweights ●
Man of the House ●
Tall Tale ●
Disney's Blizzard Beach 🐭
Water Park opens
A Goofy Movie ●
Pocahontas ●
Operation Dumbo Drop ●
A Kid in King Arthur's Court ●
The Big Green ●
Disney's Vero Beach Resort opens 🐭
Frank and Ollie ●
Toy Story (first ever full-length ● ●
CG animated feature film)
Tom and Huck ●

1980

Midnight Madness ●
The Last Flight of Noah's Ark ●

1981

The Devil and Max Devlin ●
Amy ●
The Fox and the Hound ●
Condorman ●
The Watcher in the Woods ●

1982

Night Crossing ●
Tron ●
Tex ●
EPCOT Center opens ●

1983

Trenchcoat ●
Tokyo Disney Resort and Tokyo
Disneyland open in Urayasu, Japan
The Disney Channel launches ●
Something Wicked This Way Comes ●
Never Cry Wolf ●

1988

Return to Snowy River ●
Oliver & Company ●

1989

"All New" Mickey Mouse Club ●
Disney's Hollywood Studios opens ●
Disney's Typhoon Lagoon
Water Park opens ●
Honey, I Shrunk the Kids ●
Cheetah ●
The Little Mermaid ● ★

1990

DuckTales: the Movie, Treasure ●
of the Lost Lamp
The Rescuers Down Under ●

1991

White Fang ●
Shipwrecked ●
Wild Hearts Can't Be Broken ●
The Rocketeer ●
Beauty and the Beast ● ★
Disney Vacation Club is established ●

1996

Muppet Treasure Island ●
Disney's Hilton Head ●
Island Resort opens
Homeward Bound II: ●
Lost in San Francisco
James and the Giant Peach ●
The Hunchback of Notre Dame ●
First Kid ●
D3: The Mighty Ducks ●
101 Dalmatians ●

1997

That Darn Cat ●
Jungle 2 Jungle ●
Hercules ●
George of the Jungle ●
Air Bud ●
RocketMan ●
Bear in the Big Blue House ●
Geri's Game ● ★
Flubber ●
Mr. Magoo ●

1998

Meet the Deedles ●
Disney's Animal Kingdom ●
Theme Park opens
Disney Cruise Line launches ●
the Disney Magic
Mulan ●
The Parent Trap ●
Castaway Cay opens ●
Rolie Polie Olie ●
I'll Be Home for Christmas ●
A Bug's Life ●
Mighty Joe Young ●

1999

My Favorite Martian ●
Doug's 1st Movie ●
Endurance ●
Inspector Gadget ●
Disney Cruise Line launches ●
the Disney Wonder
The Hand Behind the Mouse: ●
The Ub Iwerks Story
The Straight Story ●
Toy Story 2 ●

KEY

☙ Important events

● Documentary

● Nature documentary

● Hand-drawn animated

● Live-action

○ CG animation

● Live-action/Animated hybrid

● Stop-motion

★ Academy Award® winner

Dates refer to year of
U.S. general release

2000–2011

While continuing to innovate with technologies such as Disney Digital 3D and in-house CGI (Computer-Generated Imagery) filmmaking, the company also broadened its theme park geography. In this era, Disney officially expanded its entertainment universe with the addition of the Muppets and Pixar into its creative realm, and also created a first-of-its-kind membership group, D23: The Official Disney Fan Club.

2004

Teacher's Pet ●

Miracle ●

Disney acquires the ☙ Muppets properties

Confessions of a ● Teenage Drama Queen

Home on the Range ●

Sacred Planet ●

Around the World in 80 Days ●

America's Heart and Soul ●

The Princess Diaries 2: ● Royal Engagement

Higglytown Heroes ○

The Incredibles ○ ★

National Treasure ●

2005

Aliens of the Deep ○

The Pacifier ●

The Suite Life of Zack & Cody ●

Adventures by Disney launches ☙

Sky High ●

The Greatest Game Ever Played ●

Little Einsteins ● ○

Chicken Little ○

The Chronicles of Narnia: ● ★ The Lion, the Witch and the Wardrobe

2006

Glory Road ●

High School Musical ●

Roving Mars ○

Eight Below ●

The Shaggy Dog ●

Hannah Montana ●

The Wild ○

Disney acquires Pixar Animation ☙ Studios

Mickey Mouse Clubhouse ○

Cars ○

Pirates of the Caribbean: ● ★ Dead Man's Chest

Invincible ●

Handy Manny ○

Tim Burton's The Nightmare ● Before Christmas 3D

The Santa Clause 3: ● The Escape Clause

2007

Bridge to Terabithia ●

Meet the Robinsons ○

Pirates of the Caribbean: ● At World's End

Ratatouille ○ ★

Underdog ●

Phineas and Ferb ●

High School Musical 2 ●

The Game Plan ●

Wizards of Waverly Place ●

Enchanted ●

National Treasure: Book of Secrets ●

2000

Fantasia/2000 ●
The Tigger Movie ●
Dinosaur ●
Even Stevens ●
Disney's The Kid ●
Remember the Titans ●
Whispers: An Elephant's Tale ●
102 Dalmatians ●
The Emperor's New Groove ●

2001

Lizzie McGuire ●
Disney California Adventure Park opens ♣
The Wiggles ●
Recess: School's Out ●
Atlantis: The Lost Empire ●
The Princess Diaries ●
Tokyo DisneySea opens ♣
The Proud Family ●
Max Keeble's Big Move ●
Monsters, Inc. ● ★
For the Birds ●

2002

Snow Dogs ●
Walt Disney Studios Park ♣
(at Disneyland Paris) opens
The Rookie ●
Kim Possible ●
Lilo & Stitch ●
The Country Bears ●
Tuck Everlasting ●
The Santa Clause 2 ●
Treasure Planet ●

2003

That's So Raven ●
Ghosts of the Abyss ●
Holes ●
The Lizzie McGuire Movie ●
Finding Nemo ● ★
Pirates of the Caribbean: ●
The Curse of the Black Pearl
Freaky Friday ●
JoJo's Circus ●
Brother Bear ●
The Haunted Mansion ●
The Young Black Stallion ●

2008

Hannah Montana & Miley Cyrus: ●
Best of Both Worlds Concert
College Road Trip ●
The Chronicles of Narnia: ●
Prince Caspian
Camp Rock ●
WALL•E ● ★
Tinker Bell ●
Beverly Hills Chihuahua ●
Morning Light ●
High School Musical 3: ●
Senior Year
The Crimson Wing: Mystery of the ●
Flamingos (first released in France)
Bolt ●
Bedtime Stories ●

2009

Jonas Brothers: ●
The 3D Concert Experience
D23: The Official Disney ♣
Fan Club is formed
Race to Witch Mountain ●
Hannah Montana: The Movie ●
Earth ●
The Boys: The Sherman ●
Brothers' Story
Up ● ★
G-Force ●
Walt & El Grupo ●
Disney's A Christmas Carol ●
Old Dogs ●
The Princess and the Frog ●

2010

Alice in Wonderland ● ★
Waking Sleeping Beauty ●
Oceans ●
Prince of Persia: ●
The Sands of Time
Toy Story 3 ● ★
The Sorcerer's Apprentice ●
Secretariat ●
Shake It Up ●
Tangled ●
Tron: Legacy ●

2011

Disney Cruise Line launches ♣
the Disney Dream
Jake and the Never Land Pirates ●
Mars Needs Moms ●
African Cats: ●
Kingdom of Courage
Prom ●
Pirates of the Caribbean: ●
On Stranger Tides
Kickin' It ●
Cars 2 ●
Winnie the Pooh ●
Aulani, A Disney Resort & Spa opens ♣
Jessie ●
Minnie's Bow-Toons ●
The Muppets ● ★
Austin & Ally ●

2012–2023

The company reached into its own legacy to create new entertainment experiences, including the release of live-action fairy-tale adaptations and the introduction of streaming platform Disney+. Disney celebrated a special milestone with its 100th anniversary in 2023—reflecting on a century's worth of creativity and storytelling, and looking forward to new adventures. With many ambitious projects, the company built by Walt and Roy O. Disney marches on … to infinity and beyond!

2016

The Lion Guard ●
Zootopia ● ★
The Jungle Book ● ● ★
Alice Through The Looking Glass ●
Finding Dory ●
Piper ● ★
The BFG ●
Elena of Avalor ●
Pete's Dragon ●
Queen of Katwe ●
Moana ●

2017

Mickey Mouse Roadster Racers ●
Beauty and the Beast ● ●
Andi Mack ●
Puppy Dog Pals ●
Born in China ●
Pirates of the Caribbean: Dead Men Tell No Tales ●
Cars 3 ●
Raven's Home ●
Descendants 2 ●
DuckTales ●
Big Hero 6: The Series ●
Coco ● ★

2018

Zombies ●
A Wrinkle in Time ●
Muppet Babies ●
Incredibles 2 ●
Bao ● ★
Big City Greens ●
Fancy Nancy ●
Christopher Robin ●
Ralph Breaks the Internet ●
Mary Poppins Returns ●
Dolphin Reef ●

2019

Dumbo ●
Penguins ●
Aladdin ●
T.O.T.S. ●
Toy Story 4 ● ★
The Lion King ●
Descendants 3 ●
Maleficent: Mistress of Evil ●
Disney+ launches 🌒
Lady and the Tramp ●
Frozen 2 ●

2012

Beauty and the Beast 3D ●
Lab Rats ●
John Carter ●
Doc McStuffins ○
Disney Cruise Line launches ⚓
the Disney Fantasy
Chimpanzee ●
Gravity Falls ●
Brave ○ ★···
The Odd Life of Timothy Green ●
Frankenweenie ●
Wreck-It Ralph ○
Paperman ○ ★

2013

Sofia the First ○
Oz The Great and Powerful ●
Monsters University ○
The Lone Ranger ●
Planes ○
Frozen ○ ★···
Get a Horse! ●
Saving Mr. Banks ●
Wings of Life ○

2014

Muppets Most Wanted ●
Bears ●
Million Dollar Arm ●
Maleficent ●
Alexander and the Terrible,
Horrible, No Good,
Very Bad Day ●
Big Hero 6 ○ ★···
Feast ○ ★
Into the Woods ●

2015

Star vs. the Forces of Evil ●
Miles from Tomorrowland ●
McFarland, USA ●
Cinderella ●···
Monkey Kingdom ●
Tomorrowland ●
Inside Out ○ ★
Bunk'd ●
Descendants ●
The Good Dinosaur ○

2020

Mira, Royal Detective ○
Onward ○
Artemis Fowl ●
Mulan ●
The Wonderful World
of Mickey Mouse ●
Soul ○ ★···
Burrow ●

2021

Raya and the Last Dragon ○
Cruella ● ★
Luca ○
Monsters at Work ○
Mickey Mouse Funhouse ○
Jungle Cruise ●
Encanto ○ ★···
Diary of a Wimpy Kid ○

2022

Alice's Wonderland Bakery ○
The Proud Family:
Louder and Prouder ●
Turning Red ○···
Chip 'n Dale: Rescue Rangers ●
Lightyear ○
Disney Cruise Line launches ⚓
the Disney Wish
Pinocchio ●
Firebuds ○
Hocus Pocus 2 ○
Strange World ○
Disenchanted ●

2023

SuperKitties ○
Prom Pact ●
Peter Pan & Wendy ●
The Little Mermaid ●
Elemental ○
Haunted Mansion ●
Wish ○···

"Cartoon animation offers a medium of storytelling and visual entertainment which can bring pleasure and information to people of all ages everywhere in the world." WALT DISNEY

Animated Disney

Meet Walt

Like Thomas Edison and Charlie Chaplin, Walt had humble beginnings—and grew up to become an artistic genius. Born on December 5, 1901 in Chicago, Illinois, young Walt loved to draw cartoons, dress up in costumes, and entertain. He also made simple drawings that appeared to move as he flipped the pages—his first animation. Walt's captivation with entertainment and showmanship would combine with his love of drawing to form the foundation of his life's work. A restless innovator, Walt Disney would go on to receive hundreds of honors and citations from around the world.

FREELANCE ADVERTISING
Young Walt Disney working at his desk at Kansas City Film Ad, circa 1920.

HIGH SCHOOL CARTOONIST
The young artist made use of his talents in high school, where he drew cartoons for the McKinley High School campus magazine, *The Voice*, in Chicago, Illinois, 1918.

AN EARLY SKETCH
Another example of the young artist's work, Walt drew this lady in his sister Ruth's school book titled "My Golden School Days."

RESIDENT ARTIST
Walt served as a driver in the Red Cross Ambulance Corps in France in the immediate aftermath of World War I, for ten months. He was known as the resident artist and decorated his truck with his comical hand-drawn illustrations.

STUDIO SHORTS
Walt in Kansas City in 1922, working on one of the first Laugh-O-grams, *Jack and the Beanstalk*. Walt's goal for his first studio, Laugh-O-gram Films, Inc., was to move beyond "filler" shorts and produce animated films for movie theaters nationwide. What followed was a series of seven modernized cartoon adaptations of famous fairy tales, but sadly the studio went bankrupt.

THE DREAM BEGINS
Walt with his first motion picture camera. This photo was taken in Los Angeles shortly after his arrival in 1923.

FAMILY AFFAIR
Walt and his brother Roy photographed at Disney Brothers Cartoon Studio on Kingswell Avenue in Los Angeles, c.1924. Roy soon thought that one individual should personify the company. From then the studio bore the name Walt Disney.

The Early Years

From Walt's first live-action shorts to a lucky animated rabbit named Oswald, the future looked bright for the Disney brothers.

B y the end of 1923, Walt and Roy, his brother and business partner, had their first official studio—a tiny office, rented for $10 a month at the back of a storefront real estate office at 4651 Kingswell Avenue. They also rented a small space for outdoor shooting and bought a $200 camera. It was, as Walt would often point out, the first animation studio in California. Walt used *Alice's Wonderland*—a pilot film the young cartoonist had produced in Kansas City—to establish a distribution deal for the Alice Comedies, a series of silent animated shorts that put a live-action girl in an animated world.

FIRST PROJECT
Walt animated on several of the first Alice Comedies himself, and directed the live-action scenes. The first of the new Alice Comedies, *Alice's Day at Sea*, was delivered on December 26, 1923. With the Alice Comedies appearing in theaters, Walt invited his colleague from Kansas City, animator Ub Iwerks, to join the new Disney Studio. As he would for the rest of his career, Walt sought talents that were superior to his own, knowing such skills would improve the quality of his films.

ONE LUCKY RABBIT
With Ub Iwerks on board, Walt gave up drawing in June 1924. By late 1926, Universal Pictures asked Disney's distributor Charles Mintz for a new cartoon series starring a rabbit. He turned to Walt, who submitted sketches for a character named Oswald the Lucky Rabbit. The new cartoon

▲ Alice, played here by Virginia Davis, in Cartoonland, from the pilot *Alice's Wonderland* for the Alice Comedies (1923).

▼ Roy O. Disney (second from left) and Walt (fourth from left) pose with early employees, circa 1926: (l-r) Rollin "Ham" Hamilton, Roy, Hugh Harman, Walt, Margie Gay (second young actress to portray Alice), Rudy Ising, Ub Iwerks, Walker Harman.

◄ Publicity shot of Walt directing Alice (Margie Gay) for *Alice's Spanish Guitar* (1926) from the Alice Comedies. The series comprised 56 silent films made by Walt between 1924 and 1927.

character seemed to be lucky for Walt—he was popular, even sparking the first Disney merchandise. Oswald's creator felt secure in asking for more money in order to continue to improve both the story and the animation with each new film short. Later, after meeting with Charles Mintz in New York City, the young producer was stunned when Mintz informed him that he had hired all of Walt's animators away, with the exception of Ub Iwerks. Even more stunning was the news that Walt did not own the copyright for Oswald; Universal Studios did. Rather than accept any deals to continue with Oswald under these circumstances, Walt left the character and distributor behind. He was determined to create a new character that would be a greater success than Oswald the Lucky Rabbit.

"My brother Walt and I first went into business together [in 1923]. And he was really, in my opinion, truly a genius—creative, with great determination, singleness of purpose, and drive." ROY O. DISNEY

The Mouse Who Started it All

Created by Walt Disney and Ub Iwerks, Mickey Mouse defines the Disney brand. As Walt Disney said, "I only hope we don't lose sight of one thing—it all started with a mouse."

▼ The designer of Mickey Mouse, Ub Iwerks. Disney's first animator, Iwerks single-handedly animated the first produced Mickey Mouse cartoon.

This mini superstar with the outsized ears has caused quite a stir in sight and sounds ever since he was first unveiled in 1928. Walt created his new character on the train ride back to California after finding out he didn't own the copyright for Oswald the Lucky Rabbit. He dreamed up a lively little mouse with big round ears and wanted to name him Mortimer, but Walt's wife Lillian thought the name was too pompous. She suggested Mickey instead.

INSPIRED BY A RABBIT

Walt conferred with his top animator Ub Iwerks, who is credited with Mickey's iconic design. They immediately began work on the first produced Mickey Mouse cartoon, in which

Mickey emulated the aviation hero Charles "Lucky Lindy" Lindbergh. No distributor would take a chance on this unproven character created by an independent producer. With Mickey Mouse-like resolve—his animators always said Mickey's personality reflected Walt's own—Walt forged into

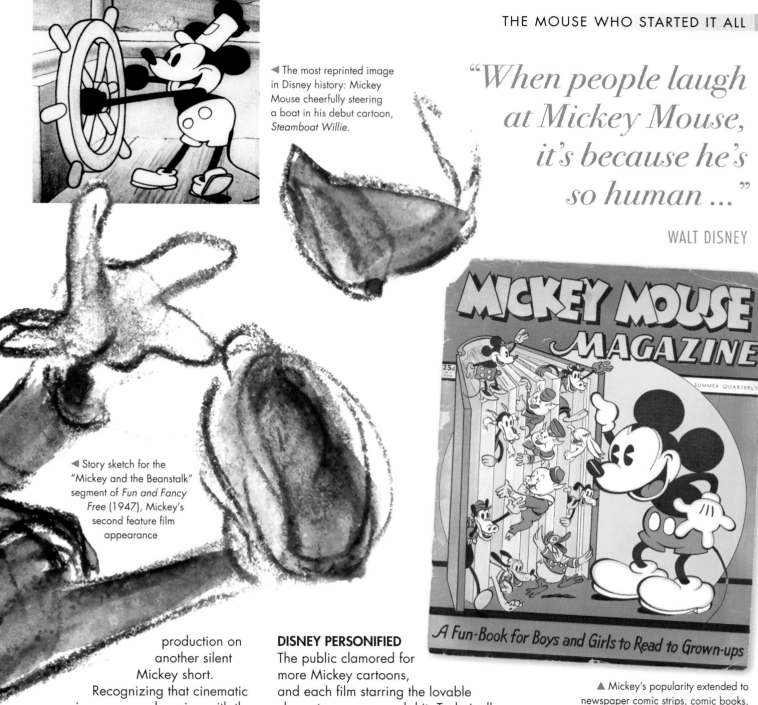

◀ The most reprinted image in Disney history: Mickey Mouse cheerfully steering a boat in his debut cartoon, *Steamboat Willie*.

"When people laugh at Mickey Mouse, it's because he's so human ..."

WALT DISNEY

◀ Story sketch for the "Mickey and the Beanstalk" segment of *Fun and Fancy Free* (1947), Mickey's second feature film appearance

▲ Mickey's popularity extended to newspaper comic strips, comic books, and his own newsstand magazine, *Mickey Mouse Magazine*. It began the summer of 1935 and in October 1935, it became a monthly periodical.

production on another silent Mickey short.

Recognizing that cinematic experiences were changing with the onset of "talkies," Walt then shifted his cartoon efforts in an innovative direction by producing his next short, *Steamboat Willie* (1928), with music and sound effects, synchronized to Mickey's antics aboard a riverboat. Walt screened *Steamboat Willie* for the New York exhibitors without attracting much initial interest. However, the manager of the Colony Theatre in New York agreed to screen the film. *Steamboat Willie* was an overwhelming success and Mickey was an overnight sensation.

DISNEY PERSONIFIED

The public clamored for more Mickey cartoons, and each film starring the lovable character was a smash hit. Technically and artistically, Mickey Mouse cartoons were far superior to other contemporary cartoons, and competing studios not only struggled to keep up, they also established animation units where none had existed—all to emulate Mickey. Mickey's cartoons were billed in lights on movie theater marquees, often above the feature film's title and live-action stars. "What—no Mickey Mouse?" became a national catchphrase signifying disappointment,

as was experienced with a theater program with no Mickey cartoon on the bill. To this day, Mickey Mouse is an internationally beloved star. Besides being the personification of everything Disney, Mickey steadfastly shines as one of the most enduring and endearing characters of our culture and times.

Mickey Magic

Mickey's beaming face is recognized around the globe, and his endearing personality has captured the imagination of generations spanning two centuries.

▲ At Walt's request, Disney artist John Hench painted this portrait of Mickey for the character's 25th anniversary in 1953. Hench also painted Mickey's official portrait for his 50th, 60th, 70th, and 75th birthdays.

► Reflecting Mickey's sunny personality, this famed "sunburst" title opened most of his animated short films from 1935 onwards.

Mickey has been a merry character in all media, from cartoons and comics to video games and apps, for nine decades and counting. It's not surprising that Walt Disney was awarded a special Academy Award® for the creation of Mickey in 1932, a testament to both Disney's creativity and Mickey's overwhelming popularity. What's behind the public passion for Mickey Mouse that has endured for almost a century? For such a modest little fellow, Mickey has a powerful design. Many artists, designers, and commentators have noted that the character has one of the most innately attractive graphic designs ever, and the simplified three-circle symbol of Mickey's head and ears is an internationally recognized icon.

GLOBAL MEDIA STAR

In addition to the 121 Mickey Mouse theatrically released cartoons, Mickey has also appeared in feature films, like *Fantasia* (1940), which had its world premiere in the same New York theater as *Steamboat Willie* (1928) 12 years earlier. Since Walt Disney was the first Hollywood heavy-hitter to enter the burgeoning medium of television, Mickey was naturally one of TV's earliest stars. Inspired by the Mickey Mouse Clubs of the 1930s—the club met every Saturday for an afternoon of cartoons and games in local theaters—Walt created the *Mickey Mouse Club* television series in 1955. Mickey's evergreen popularity made the show an instant hit. In 1956, viewership was at more than 14 million, with more than one-third of that audience made up of adults. Mickey's timeless cartoons were showcased in the daily Mouse cartoon, with more people seeing them in one day than during their original theatrical releases. But Mickey's talents don't end there. He is also a recording star, with a hit platinum-selling album, *Mickey Mouse Disco*, released in 1979, and the groove continued with a companion short of past musical cartoon moments cut together to a disco soundtrack in 1980.

◀ On November 13, 1978, Mickey became the first animated character to be honored with a star on the Hollywood Walk of Fame.

▼ Mickey made his Disney animated feature film premiere playing the role of the Sorcerer's Apprentice in the original *Fantasia* (1940).

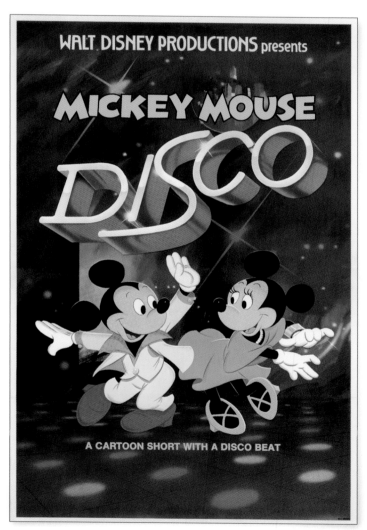

WALT DISNEY PRODUCTIONS presents

MICKEY MOUSE DISCO

A CARTOON SHORT WITH A DISCO BEAT

▲ Mickey and Minnie groove their way across the dance floor on the promotional poster for the short crafted to highlight the album *Mickey Mouse Disco*.

Modern Era Mickey

Whatever the platform on which the happy Mickey Mouse pops up, he always remains his audience-pleasing self.

▲ Mickey Mouse as featured in the *Mickey Mouse Club* (1989) logo on The Disney Channel, aiming for older audiences than previous renditions.

The magic of Walt Disney's star shines through cultural and technological changes year after year, show after show, bringing laughter and heartwarming entertainment through Mickey's charming personality and adventures.

MOUSE OF ALL MEDIUMS
In more recent times, Disney fans have enjoyed the computer-animated *Mickey Mouse Clubhouse* (2006) on the Disney Channel, *Mickey Mouse Mixed-Up Adventures* (2017) and *Mickey Mouse Funhouse* (2021) on Disney Junior, and also the Emmy® Award-winning *Mickey Mouse* series (2013) that has the slapstick feel of classic Mickey Mouse, combined with contemporary direction and pacing. In 2014, Mickey Mouse received his first Oscar® nomination in nearly 20 years with the groundbreaking hand-drawn CG-animated short, *Get a Horse!* (2013) directed by Lauren MacMullan. Although his look may change slightly when in 2D or CG universes, the joyful innocence and good-heartedness of Mickey Mouse plays through all his fun-loving episodes.

"Mickey was simply a little personality assigned to the purposes of laughter." WALT DISNEY

◄ Mickey's head is made from three circles, making him easy to animate and a perfect logo.

◄ Mickey and Donald float through the skies in the *Mickey Mouse Clubhouse* series.

STREAM OF MOUSINESS

The Wonderful World of Mickey Mouse launched on Disney+ in 2020, through which fans could enjoy classic Mickey entertainment on the screen of their choosing, anytime and anywhere. In 2022, the documentary film *Mickey: The Story of a Mouse* premiered at the SXSW festival and later aired on Disney+, sharing the beloved character's history and evolution, with the new animated short *Mickey in a Minute* included.

▲ Minnie hires Mickey to manage a rolling herd in the Wild West of Big Thunder Valley in "Cheese Wranglers," the first episode of the first season of *The Wonderful World of Mickey Mouse.*

◄ Minnie and Mickey are aflutter with Minnie's avian photography quest in the "Birdwatching" episode of *The Wonderful World of Mickey Mouse.*

Mickey's Friends

A popular character like Mickey is never going to be short of friends.

▲ Donald's leading lady is Daisy Duck, seen in this story sketch for the Noah's Ark "Pomp and Circumstance" segment of *Fantasia/2000* (2000).

Minnie Mouse charmed her way into the hearts of both Mickey Mouse and audiences when she debuted in *Steamboat Willie* (1928). Her companionship with Mickey through the years since has made them an endearing duo, but she has also owned the spotlight in her own specials and series through the decades, including *Disney's Totally Minnie* (1988) and *Minnie's Bow-Toons* (2011).

A MOUSE'S BEST FRIEND
Mickey's canine costar—the character who would go on to be known as Pluto—was once a pet named Rover and belonged to Minnie, not Mickey.

He later became Mickey's pet once and for all, and the pooch was most likely named Pluto the Pup in honor of the then-newly discovered planet. It was master animator Norm Ferguson who made Pluto the thinking man's mutt, and animated the pantomime pooch's thought processes and inner life. Pluto has starred in comics, games, and his own cartoons, alongside Mickey in the Academy Award®-winning short film *Lend a Paw* (1941) and has appeared in

numerous films, series, and other shorts over the course of his many dog years on screen.

FAMOUS FOWL
Donald Duck had an unusual start to his career. He was hatched June 9, 1934 with the release of the Silly Symphony, *The Wise Little Hen*. Walt Disney created the Duck character around the distinctive voice performed by Clarence "Ducky" Nash. Universally acclaimed, the foul-tempered fowl has movie fans

◄ Goofy, Mickey, and Donald attempt to escape from trouble in a cartoon.

◀ A story sketch shows Donald, Mickey, and Goofy working together as a comedy trio.

▼ Right from the start, Minnie Mouse played, performed, and romanced with her sweetheart and leading man, Mickey.

"Mickey is ... an impresario, sharing the spotlight with many new personalities. Some of them ... have gone on to become stars in their own right."

WALT DISNEY

in 76 countries, readers who have followed his daily comic strip in 100 international newspapers, friends who have read his comic books published in 47 nations, and television families who have watched him in 29 countries.

CLUMSY DOG?

Like Donald Duck, the lanky, lovable Goofy started with a voice, or in this case, a laugh. Disney story artist Pinto Colvig came up with a novelty laugh that inspired Walt Disney to create a hound in *Mickey's Revue* (1932). In addition to helping Mickey in his comic-book and comic-strip adventures, Goofy has also starred in more than 50 cartoons of his own. He has joined

Mickey and Donald to form one of the screen's funniest teams in many shorts, films, and games through the years.

▼ Mickey's loyal pet Pluto often took a starring role in his films, such as *Society Dog Show* (1939).

Short But Symphonic

An orchestration of glittering color, winsome characters, and unforgettable music, the Silly Symphonies raised the art of animation to new and harmonious heights.

▲ Walt Disney's Silly Symphony superstars—Fiddler, Practical, and Fifer Pig—from one of the most popular cartoons ever produced.

"We used [the Silly Symphonies] to test and perfect the color and animation techniques we employed later in full-length feature pictures ..." WALT DISNEY

Scene I
First pig building straw house.

Scene II
Second pig building house of sticks

Scene III
Third pig building house of brick

◄ The three little pigs are a study in contrasts—and contrasting homes of straw, sticks, and bricks—in these story sketches.

The Silly Symphonies were born of Walt Disney's unending drive to improve and innovate. Mickey Mouse was an overnight sensation, but the ever-imaginative producer was not content to simply ride the coattails of Mickey's popularity. He immediately began thinking of a new series of cartoons that would give him the artistic freedom to create any number of animated personalities, without being tied down to one continuing character.

NEW POSSIBILITIES
Walt's first musical director Carl Stalling, later famed for his compositions for the *Looney Tunes* cartoons, suggested a new series of shorts where music would be the main ingredient. Originally, the shorts were to feature inanimate objects coming to life to the rhythm of the soundtrack melodies, but they soon evolved into something more. The first Silly Symphony—a series title that Walt himself dreamed up—was *The Skeleton Dance* (1929), a one-of-a-kind animated musical unlike anything seen or heard on the screen before. These early mini-musical extravaganzas, such as *Autumn* (1930), were well received, but the series really struck the right note with the addition of color. The production of *Flowers and Trees* (1932) coincided with the perfection of the full-color

three-strip Technicolor® process. Many in Hollywood were uninterested, but Walt was thrilled with the possibilities. At great cost, the completed work on *Flowers and Trees* was scrapped and the film was redone in breathtaking color, winning Walt Disney his first Academy Award®.

AWARD TRIUMPHS

The Silly Symphonies reached a new level of excellence when *Three Little Pigs* (1933) became a phenomenon. Boasting a hit song, "Who's Afraid of the Big Bad Wolf?" and three distinct personalities, whom Walt considered to be a quantum leap in character

animation, the short started an excitement matched only by Mickey. Other hits followed, featuring ever more sophisticated music, as in *The Grasshopper and the Ants* (1934), and vibrant new personalities such as the put-upon pachyderm in *Elmer Elephant* (1936). The series dominated the Academy Awards®, winning the Best Animated Short Film Oscar® every year until the Silly Symphonies were phased out in 1939. Many innovations were introduced and perfected in these special animated shorts, making possible Walt's future animated triumphs.

▲ This story sketch for *The Goddess of Spring* (1934), a precursor for *Snow White and the Seven Dwarfs*, shows Disney's early attempts at depicting the human form.

▲ As seen in this *Good Housekeeping* magazine adaption, *The Wise Little Hen* (1934) hatched a new star—Donald Duck.

◄ One of the most elaborate of the Silly Symphonies, *The Old Mill* (1937) was a cinematic tone poem and the first animated film to utilize Disney's revolutionary multiplane camera.

A Cartoon Family

With the huge success of Mickey and his pals, Disney animators were inspired to extend his family and friends.

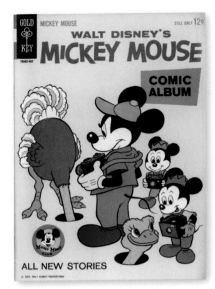

▲ Mickey's nephews, Morty and Ferdie, frequently appeared in the comics, as in this cover for *Mickey Mouse* #95 (1964), drawn by Paul Murry.

Every star needs supporting players—and the popularity of not only Mickey, but also of Minnie Mouse, Donald Duck, and Goofy, inspired Walt and his artists to create a gang of new characters. Before Donald and Goofy, Mickey had two pals that evolved out of the barnyard origins of some of his earliest screen successes. Gossipy Clarabelle Cow quickly evolved to become the confidante of Mickey and especially Minnie. Clarabelle was often paired with Horace Horsecollar, who started

▼ Donald's frequent companions in adventure: his outrageously wealthy uncle, Scrooge McDuck, and his quick-thinking nephews, Huey, Dewey, and Louie

out as an actual barnyard equine, but soon became Mickey's reliable buddy. Clarabelle and Horace are on hand when Mickey's friends get together in cartoons such as *Mickey's Birthday Party* (1942), but it is in comics that these small-town friends make most of their neighborly appearances.

MICKEY'S NEPHEWS
Like Clarabelle and Horace, Mickey's nephews, Morty (Mortimer) and Ferdie (Ferdinand) Fieldmouse, had a limited screen career compared to their appearances in comics.

Their only screen appearance was in *Mickey's Steam-Roller* (1934), but they first featured in the *Mickey Mouse* comic strip on September 18, 1932.

TALES ABOUT A DUCK
Since Mickey had two nephews, Donald had to go one better. Huey, Dewey, and Louie debuted in the "Silly Symphony" Sunday comic feature (which starred Donald at that time) on October 17, 1937. Soon after, the dauntless ducklings appeared in their first screen cartoon, *Donald's Nephews* (1938), and have been a part of the quarrelsome quacker's life ever since. Together with Donald's nephews, Scrooge McDuck starred in the *DuckTales* TV series in 1987 and again in 2017.

▲ Chip and Dale in a clean-up animation drawing by Bill Justice for *All in a Nutshell* (1949)

"One of the greatest satisfactions in our work here at the studio is the warm relationship that exists within our cartoon family." WALT DISNEY

The "richest duck in the world" was first introduced as a foil for Donald in a 1947 comic-book story, "Christmas on Bear Mountain." A perfect sparring partner for Donald, the miserly duck was also a veritable gold mine of comedy and excitement. In many comic-book escapades, Uncle Scrooge, Donald, and the nephews form an intrepid band of globetrotting adventurers. Though they first appeared with Mickey and Pluto in 1943, Chip and Dale became the perfect irritants for Donald Duck. The chipmunks appeared in 24 theatrical cartoons and starred in their own TV series *Chip 'n' Dale Rescue Rangers*, that premiered in 1989, as well as a hybrid feature film on Disney+ in 2022.

▲ A story sketch of two of Mickey's earliest and most comical cohorts, Clarabelle Cow and Horace Horsecollar

◀ Counterparts to Huey, Dewey, and Louie, April, May, and June are the nieces of Daisy Duck, seen here in a story from a 1961 issue of *Daisy Duck's Diary* comic book, drawn by Carl Barks.

Magic Mirror

With the success of Mickey Mouse and the Silly Symphonies, Walt set out to create an entirely new form of cinema— the feature-length animated film.

▲ Early concept art explored different designs for Disney's first princess.

As successful as Walt's animated shorts were, they didn't artistically satisfy him for long. In deciding to produce an animated feature, he envisioned not just a long "cartoon," but also an entertainment experience that would surpass what even the finest live-action motion picture could achieve. With the romance of Snow White and the Prince, the menace of the Queen in disguise, and the sympathetic, comical Dwarfs, *Snow White and the Seven Dwarfs* (1937) was, Walt believed, the perfect story. The human characters presented the animators with their greatest challenge. As Disney artist Woolie Reitherman later pointed out, no one at Disney had ever animated a realistic girl, but Walt was determined to create a believable fairy-tale princess. He pioneered a landmark method for training and preparing his animators by sending them to art classes to study human form and movement. He also hired artists schooled in traditional painting and sculpture. The artists continually sought ways to bring the princess to life: a subtle but effective touch is the rosy glow on Snow White's cheeks.

▼ In the original Brothers Grimm fairy tale, the Dwarfs were anonymous figures, but Walt gave each of his Dwarfs a name that would explain his personality: (l-r) Sneezy, Dopey, Bashful, Happy, Sleepy, Grumpy, and the leader, Doc.

"Of all the characters in the fairy tales I loved Snow White the best, and when I planned my first full-length feature, she inevitably was the heroine." WALT DISNEY

▲ A quaint cottage in the woods is shown in this background painting by Samuel Armstrong.

DRAWING DWARFS

Walt set out to establish his Dwarfs as seven distinct, vivid characters. The filmmakers spent hours discussing everything about the Dwarfs—how they would move and act, and even how they would move their hands. The animators managed to convey personality and attitude just through the shape of the body and posture.

MOVIE MAGIC

Walt and his staff just met their deadline of Christmas 1937 and two prints of the completed *Snow White and the Seven Dwarfs* were delivered to the theater mere hours before the premiere. After four years of painstaking work and a then record-shattering $1.5 million budget,

Disney's ambitious film was unveiled on December 21, 1937. Critics raved and audiences flocked to see *Snow White*, making it the top box-office hit up until that time.

The final scenes of *Snow White and the Seven Dwarfs* include a handsome prince, "True Love's Kiss," a magnificent castle, and the triumph of good over evil. Walt Disney had been convinced that the magic and romance of *Snow White and the Seven Dwarfs* made it the perfect story. Each of these elements would continue to appear in many successsful Disney movies for decades to come.

A Sumptuous Epic

▲ Watercolor pre-production painting by Gustaf Tenggren featuring early designs of the kindly Geppetto and the magical Blue Fairy.

▼ Watercolor pre-production painting of the Italian village setting by Gustaf Tenggren

Pinocchio weaves the tale of a little wooden boy who comes to life in a wondrously wrought world. At the time of its release, it was the most elaborate animated movie ever made.

With *Pinocchio* (1940), Walt Disney and his artists set out to surpass the success of *Snow White and the Seven Dwarfs* and in so doing they created what many consider to be the ultimate in the art of animation. The quaint storybook setting inspired much intricate detail in this film's lavish production design, from the ornate clocks and toys in Geppetto's workshop right down to the cobblestones in the crooked streets of Pinocchio's village. Cost was no object as Walt poured a sizable portion of the profits from *Snow White* into this new movie. The visionary filmmaker sought an unprecedented level of animated extravagance as Albert Hurter, Gustaf Tenggren, and other celebrated masters of fantasy created the intricate visual style for *Pinocchio*, with

an emphasis on old world atmosphere. Sculptors crafted three-dimensional models of the characters and many of the props, including the Pleasure Island stagecoach, Stromboli's birdcage, and the ribcage of Monstro the whale.

A REAL BOY AND HIS CONSCIENCE

Such was Walt's tireless quest for perfection that he discarded six months of animation and story work because he felt the burgeoning project lacked emotion and warmth. The main problem was Pinocchio himself. Reflecting the character as portrayed in the original book by Carlo Collodi, Disney's first version of the wooden puppet was a sticklike, unsympathetic, and disobedient child with hands like paddles and a cocky personality. In February 1939, animator Milt Kahl designed a cute and rounded character—more an innocent little boy than a marionette. Once the lovable child was drawn it was a simple matter to add the wooden joints and nails that made him a puppet. Walt knew that a guileless main character—literally "born yesterday," thanks to the Blue Fairy's magic—needed a guide, and so the master storyteller took a talking cricket (squashed in the original book by the ill-tempered puppet) and made him Pinocchio's conscience. Walt's directive to animator Ward Kimball was to design a cute cricket named

▲ Final frame showing the little wooden boy and his cricket conscience.

Jiminy. After 14 or so different versions, the artist finally eliminated all insect appendages and came up with a tiny, bald, humanlike character, wearing a tailcoat suggesting folded wings and with two hairs evocative of antennae. Today, with its endearing characters and sumptuous settings, the movie is still considered by many to be a quintessential Disney Animation film.

> *"... technically and artistically [Pinocchio] was superior. It indicated that we had grown considerably as craftsmen ..."* WALT DISNEY

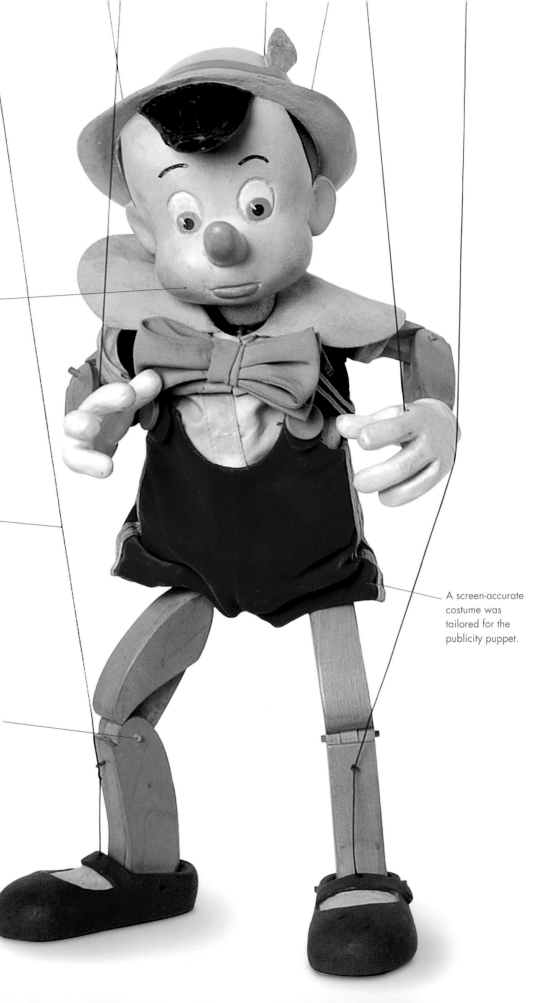

PUBLICITY PUPPET
Created to be a real working puppet, this Pinocchio marionette could be articulated by Disney artists in publicity photos using some of the techniques taught to them by model maker Bob Jones, who was also a puppeteer.

Disney's ink and paint artists applied authentic colors to the Pinocchio puppet's face.

Skilled puppeteer Bob Jones helped determine exactly where to place the strings, ensuring that the marionette could be moved in a myriad of actions.

A screen-accurate costume was tailored for the publicity puppet.

As real as a marionette in any puppet show, Pinocchio had wooden joints in his arms and legs that allowed him to wave, walk, and dance.

A Marionette Discovered

In creating *Pinocchio*, Walt wanted his artists to capture the movement of an actual wooden puppet. Character Model Department artists Wah Ming Chang, Charles Cristadoro, and Bob Jones crafted a 3D model of the marionette movie star, which was then brought to colorful life by painter Helen Nerbovig. Jones was a skilled puppeteer and trained the directing animator Frank Thomas to properly manipulate a marionette. Jones also created a fully functional Pinocchio puppet to help publicize the new film. In 2003, the marionette was discovered in near-perfect condition in a homemade plywood cabinet—covered over the years by telephone cables—built into the basement at The Walt Disney Studios in Burbank. Today the priceless figure has a new home in the Walt Disney Animation Research Library.

WALT AND PINOCCHIO
Just prior to the premiere of *Pinocchio* in 1940, Walt Disney put the working marionette crafted by model maker Bob Jones and ink and paint artist Helen Nerbovig through its paces for the publicity cameras. For many years, this photograph was the only evidence that the puppet had existed.

▲ *Fantasia* used new techniques, including special paints and mechanical devices, to create worlds like the undersea realm in "The Nutcracker Suite."

Music in Motion

Classic animation and classical music combine to form *Fantasia*, a spellbinding motion picture of timeless artistry.

A sight-and-sound celebration of music and artistry, *Fantasia* (1940) began in late 1937 when Walt first considered Dukas's "The Sorcerer's Apprentice" as a deluxe short to star Mickey Mouse. The concept of this ambitious short soon evolved into an entire feature consisting of classical pieces as interpreted by the Disney artists in a mix of intriguing art styles, that were dictated by each piece's unique

◄ *Fantasia* debuted in 1940 at the Broadway Theatre, a mere twelve years after *Steamboat Willie* premiered there in 1928.

symphonic soundtrack. The project was once known as the "Concert Feature" but later transitioned to the title "Fantasia," literally meaning "an unconventional music piece."

INNOVATIVE ANIMATION

Walt and his artists listened to the world's most acclaimed classical music, eventually selecting seven additional pieces. From innovative abstraction in "Toccata and Fugue in D Minor" to the hilarious corps de ballet of hippos and elephants in Ponchielli's "The Dance of the Hours," *Fantasia* overflows with unsurpassed artistry. In "The Nutcracker Suite" by Tchaikovsky, tumbling flowers swirl, glide, and pirouette across the surface of water like a troupe of ballerinas. "The Pastoral Symphony" is an interpretation of life in mythical ancient Greece. It features centaurs frolicking in the shadow of Mount Olympus and unicorns—perfect subjects for Disney animation's unique ability to bring anything to life. Walt made a bold choice selecting Stravinsky's "Rite of

Spring." For the innovative impresario, the avant-garde composition inspired visions of nothing less than the formation of the earth and the coming of dinosaurs. The Disney animation effects artists animated both the real and the fantastical—bubbling lava, delicate sprites, and intricate snowflakes. In the climatic combination of Moussorgsky's "Night on Bald Mountain" and Schubert's "Ave Maria," there are creeping shadows and ghostly specters, as well as glowing candles in a mist-filled forest.

INTO THE FUTURE

This magnificent animated feature was honored with a special Academy Award® for its sound, which recognized *Fantasia* as a work that widened the scope of the motion picture as an art form.

"In a profession that has been an unending voyage of discovery in the realms of color, sound, and motion, Fantasia represents our most exciting adventure." WALT DISNEY

▶ The Disney artists studied prima ballerinas to create "The Dance of the Hours" concept art, including this study of dancing hippos and elephants.

The Orchestra Plays On

Walt had intended to turn *Fantasia* into an ongoing event, re-releasing it every year with new segments. His vision was finally realized with *Fantasia/2000*, a spectacular follow-up spearheaded by Walt's nephew, Roy E. Disney.

▲ The beauty of the Arctic, in both water and sky, is featured in a "Pines of Rome" color key for *Fantasia/2000*.

▲ *Fantasia/2000* played on IMAX screens up to eight stories in height, making for an even grander cinematic experience.

Continuing the creative walk in his uncle's footsteps, Roy E. Disney became Vice Chairman of the Board in 1984, overseeing Walt Disney Feature Animation, and knew from a young age that he wanted to continue the *Fantasia* experiment. After nine years in the making, *Fantasia/2000* (2000) premiered with seven new musical segments, as well as "The Sorcerer's Apprentice" from the original film, interwoven with the symphonic, cinematic journey. The film captured the emotional artistic variation and experimentation of the original *Fantasia* while also celebrating the fresh artistic talents, styles, innovation, and excitement of the new century. *Fantasia/2000* paid homage to the roots of the Disney creative spirit with Mickey Mouse as a central star in the very film that was meant to give him new popularity in the 1940s.

A CINEMATIC ENCORE
The movie begins with Beethoven's "Symphony No. 5," featuring abstract 3D computer animation that instantly immerses the audience in a world of color, and a struggle between light and dark. Next is "Pines of Rome" by Ottorino Respighi, offering a softer computer-generated look through majestic animation of whales. Following is "Rhapsody in Blue" by George Gershwin, a 2D visual adventure inspired by the illustrative style of Al Hirschfeld; next is "Piano Concerto No. 2, Allegro, Opus 102" by Dimitri Shostakovich, which portrays the dramatic story of a toy soldier with a broken leg, the beautiful ballerina he loves, and a battle with an evil jack-in-the-box. "Carnival of the Animals" by Camille Saint-Saëns brings humor through a yo-yoing flamingo that rebels against its flock; following is the classic "The Sorcerer's Apprentice" by Paul Dukas starring Mickey Mouse in true vintage animation. The symphonic adventure continues with "Pomp and Circumstance, Marches 1, 2, 3, and 4," by Edward Elgar, featuring Donald Duck as an assistant to Noah on his Ark, in a segment that gives a nod to the 1940s style of cartoons. The film concludes with "Firebird Suite (1919 Version)" by Igor Stravinsky, portrayed in a wondrously sprite-ful adventure in nature. The individual segments were introduced by

▲ Abstract art and moving music combine for a suspenseful short in the "Symphony No. 5," segment of *Fantasia/2000*.

▲ A supernova allows whales to take their graceful swim to new heights in *Fantasia/2000*'s "Pines of Rome" segment.

▲ Director Eric Goldberg adapted an early concept about ostriches and yo-yos from Disney legend Joe Grant into a more colorful take with flamingos in "Carnival of the Animals" for *Fantasia/2000*.

▲ Donald Duck had big responsibility on an even bigger boat, and his hard work paid off with a reunion with Daisy in *Fantasia/2000*'s "Pomp and Circumstance" segment, as directed by Francis Glebas.

celebrities Steve Martin, Bette Midler, Quincy Jones, James Earl Jones, Penn & Teller, and Angela Lansbury alongside others.

LIVE ORCHESTRA EXPERIENCE

Launched as the 38th Disney animated feature, *Fantasia/2000* premiered with a live performance at Carnegie Hall in New York City, and went global with a prestigious international concert tour through London, Paris, Tokyo, and Los Angeles. Audiences were also able to enjoy the film in the super-screen format of IMAX in select locations during its theatrical run.

◀ The artistry of Dalí was translated into a Disney short by John Hench who worked directly with Dalí in 1946 and was finally given the green light to finish *Destino* 57 years later. It was set to music written by songwriter Armando Domínguez.

FANTASIA CONTINUED

Disney artists completed work on other musical segments in anticipation of another *Fantasia* project, but these pieces were released as stand-alone short films, instead of being shelved for years awaiting that feature. These short musical films include *One by One* (2004), *The Little Matchgirl* (2006), *Destino* (2003, but 58 years in the making,) and *Lorenzo* (2004, with initial production efforts launched in 1943.)

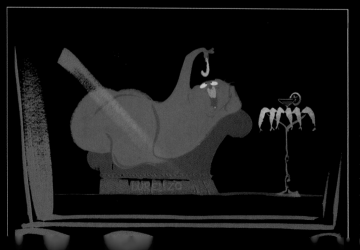

◀ Director Mike Gabriel brought Joe Grant's tale of a cat who tangos with his tail to life, choreographed to the soundtrack of Juan José Mosalini's "Bordoneo y 900" in *Lorenzo*.

Little Elephant, Big Heart

Dumbo tells the heartwarming tale of the world's one and only flying elephant.

O ne day in 1940, Walt Disney stopped Ward Kimball in the Studio parking lot to tell him the story of an outcast baby elephant with oversized ears— and the animator immediately knew that the simple story had great cartoon heart, held together with the great fantasy of a flying elephant. To create the colorful circus backdrop, Walt turned to big-top aficionados Bill Peet (story artist) and Herb Ryman (pre-production artist) who had both painted circus scenes. All the *Dumbo* (1941) artists went on a field trip to the celebrated Cole Bros. Circus where they studied the performers and animals.

▲ The circus provides a vibrant setting for *Dumbo*.

▶ Dumbo takes flight with Timothy along for the ride.

▲ Story sketch of Dumbo and his sidekick Timothy from 1941

BUBBLE
BUBBLE

CREATING CUTENESS
Animator John Lounsbery was the first to draw the eponymous big-eared elephant with caricatured human-babylike features. Many were surprised when Walt assigned Bill Tytla as the baby pachyderm's directing animator, as Bill was best known for animating powerful characters such as the demonic Chernabog in *Fantasia*. Bill shut himself in his office for two weeks and emerged with the charming little character, whose sincere expressions and mannerisms the animator had observed in his own uninhibited two-year-old son.

A CHATTY SIDEKICK
To guide the oppressed Dumbo through his trials and tribulations, the Disney artists came up with the delightful conceit of a mouse—traditionally seen as an elephant's enemy—as Dumbo's best pal. The chatty rodent—a circus show mouse called Timothy—talked enough for both himself

and his voiceless friend. The Disney artists had trouble finding the perfect voice for Timothy until Walt advised them to simply look for a voice that made them laugh. The filmmakers cast Hollywood character actor Ed Brophy, well-known for playing comical crooks, who also served as the real-life model for tough but tenderhearted Timothy.

A TRUE TRIUMPH

One of the film's highlights is the brilliantly conceived and innovative "Pink Elephants on Parade" sequence. Years ahead of its time in color, form, and surreal imagery, this musical number imaginatively employed the unbounded nature of the art of animation—for example, an elephant entirely made from heads and one made from nothing but trunks. Produced in the remarkably short time of only a year and a half, *Dumbo* reflected the confidence Walt and his entire staff felt in this project. The master storyteller felt the joy radiating from the film was a reflection of the happiness he and his artists experienced in creating it.

"Dumbo was a fun picture to make and the result is a fun picture to watch." WALT DISNEY

▼ The colorful Casey Jr. circus train transporting Dumbo and company.

Animal Artistry

The dramatic story and gentle animal characters of *Bambi* challenged Walt Disney and his artists to take the art of animation to breathtaking new heights of wonder and beauty.

▲ Concept art by Tyrus Wong from 1942

▼ Animal artist Rico Lebrun guides *Bambi* artists as they sketch a live deer.

Adapted from Felix Salten's novel, *Bambi: A Life in the Woods*, Walt Disney's sublime animated feature tells the story of a young deer's coming of age with his friends, Thumper the rabbit and Flower the skunk. When *Bambi* (1942) development began in 1936, Walt started to prepare a team of hand-selected artists who would ultimately spend six years working on the film. The ever-imaginative impresario brought in expert animal draftsman Rico Lebrun to train the *Bambi* artists in animal anatomy and locomotion. A pair of four-month-old fawns was brought to live at the Studio for the animators to study. Additional creatures, including birds, squirrels, chipmunks, and rabbits, also served as live models.

VISUAL POETRY

To create a realistic yet stylized forest environment for *Bambi*, Walt enlisted the talents of conceptual artist Tyrus Wong. Wong created hundreds of subtle and evocative inspirational sketches that suggested moods and themes. Walt recognized that Wong's poetic style had a great influence throughout the film especially within staging, backgrounds, and color imagery. He brought a visually poetic sensibility to the film's art direction with his impressionistic paintings and styling sketches, suggesting the mood and

"There was a need for subtlety in our animation and the need for a more lifelike type of animation." WALT DISNEY

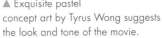

▲ Exquisite pastel concept art by Tyrus Wong suggests the look and tone of the movie.

▲ Final frame from the movie with Bambi, Flower, and Thumper in the forest

color of the setting rather than elaborate detail. Wong's goal was to create the atmosphere of the forest.

HEARTWARMING CHARACTERS

Two of *Bambi*'s most beloved stars were not in the original book. Flower the skunk was introduced into the movie by Walt during an early story conference. Thumper was originally to be only one of the children of a central character named Mr. Hare. However, Thumper's role as Bambi's best friend kept expanding and the storyline was adapted to fit the appeal of this emerging character. The young

rabbit's personality really took off when four-year-old Peter Behn was cast as the character's voice. The young voice actor's unaffected acting helped to turn the enthusiastic rabbit into a scene-stealing star. Thumper soon not only displaced Mr. Hare, but also became the young deer's guide to the natural wonders of the forest, taking over the role from Bambi's mother. Walt Disney felt the personalities in *Bambi* were, as he put it, "pure gold." According to two of the film's supervising animators, Frank Thomas and Ollie Johnston, *Bambi* was Walt's favorite of all his films.

▲ Ilene Woods, the voice of Cinderella, rehearses before a recording session.

Tick Tock Turnaround

Cinderella proves that hope and kindness triumph over evil.

From the moment Cinderella awakens in her attic room and sings to her adoring animal friends, the lonely scullery maid wins hearts with her grace and kindness. Cinderella is soft-spoken and gentle, but there's more to her than first meets the eye. Despite the humiliating treatment she receives from her jealous stepsisters and evil stepmother, Cinderella is anything but weak-willed and dares to stand up to her stepmother, insisting that she, too, should attend the royal ball.

A DREAM TO REALITY
To create a character who audiences would root for, animators Marc Davis and Eric Larson knew *Cinderella* (1950) had to make its namesake star's every emotion, expression, and movement believable. They filmed live-action footage of 18-year-old actress Helene Stanley acting out the entire Cinderella story, then used the footage for inspiration. Ilene Woods' rich tones, which Walt once described as a "fairy-tale voice," gave Cinderella's personality a warmth and confidence, helping to create a princess who deserves the magic and love that transforms her life from drudgery to a dream come true.

DONNING THE DRESS
Walt and his team knew that costuming was an important part of a character's performance, and great details went into portraying Cinderella in both her everyday and belle-of-the-ball outfits. Marc Davis, Mary Blair, and other artists contributed a plethora of designs to the development of Cinderella's diverse wardrobe.

A DELICATE DANCE
Animators who were assigned realistic human character scenes learned a great deal about how to portray accurate motion by watching reference footage of live actors. It was important for animator Eric Larson to express authentic human motion in order to convey the charming romance between Cinderella and her Prince, especially in their whirlwind dance scenes—as opposed to how artists

▲ 1948 concept art by Marc Davis shows different angles of Cinderella in her work dress.

might animate comedic characters in the broader "squash and stretch" range of exaggerated motion.

PUMPKIN PROCESS

While the idea of a fairy godmother turning a pumpkin into a glass coach is a magical concept perfect for the animation medium, the artistic reality of making it happen was a daunting challenge that Disney talent delivered on with majesty. Layout artist Ken O'Connor sculpted a physical model of the carriage to serve as reference for drawing the creative vehicle from any angle. After animation drawings were made, ink and paint artists crafted a glass enclosed coach— and the ball-bound beauty within it— in color, taking cues from concept art. And the end result is iconic cinematic history of which any fairy godmother (and animation crew) should be proud.

▲ Mary Blair brings her romantic and whimsical eye to the palatial world of *Cinderella* in concept art.

"Even though Cinderella had her sad moments, she still stood strong all the way through." MARC DAVIS

◀ Ethereal concept painting conveys the fairy-tale magic of *Cinderella*.

Fly By Night

Walt Disney recognized that to make *Peter Pan*, animation would be the perfect medium to portray the J. M. Barrie play about the boy who never grows up.

Extensive live-action reference footage was shot to inspire the animators, with the voice actors performing their roles. The story's fantasy called for the artists to animate the characters flying. To indicate high-spirited Peter Pan's power of flight, veteran Disney artist Milt Kahl animated the character as if he were floating in midair. *Peter Pan* (1953) was proof that the Disney artists had become expert at animating human characters. Even the villainous Captain Hook jumped from storybook character to classic cinema villain legend, coming to life through the animation talents of Frank Thomas and the voice skills of veteran radio actor Hans Conried.

AWAY WE GO

Peter Pan was one of Walt Disney's favorite stories, but when he finally

▲ Development for *Peter Pan* began in the late 1930s, as seen in this early concept art.

gained the rights to make the movie, he had a hard time deciding exactly how Peter should be portrayed, both in terms of appearance and character. Walt eventually settled on a merry—but mischievous—individual who could

◄ Mary Blair's concept art uses light and abstract shapes to bring magic to the world of Peter Pan and Never Land.

▼ Mermaid Lagoon is swimmingly beautiful, as painted by Mary Blair in this concept art.

"Fantasy, if it's really convincing, can't become dated, for the simple reason that it represents a flight into a dimension that lies beyond the reach of time." WALT DISNEY

◄ Jake is ready for a swashbuckling adventure in *Jake and the Never Land Pirates*.

◄ Peter Pan and Captain Hook are at odds again in *Return to Never Land*.

▼ The ever-youthful Peter Pan continues the fun with Jane, daughter of Wendy, in *Return to Never Land*.

fly without wings. Viewers would be enthralled when they watched the fairylike Peter Pan take Wendy, John, and Michael Darling swooping and soaring over the spires of London, heading toward Never Land.

THE FUN OF FLIGHT CONTINUES

Although some of the scenes and themes of *Peter Pan* seemed more dark and sinister than prior Disney animation films, the level of fantasy and drama appealed greatly to audiences then and for generations to come. In more recent times, viewers have enjoyed the sequel *Return to Never Land* (2002), the television series *Jake and the Never Land Pirates* (2011), and the live-action film *Peter Pan & Wendy* (2023).

The World's Favorite Fairy

◀ Tink's mischievous spirit shines in a clean-up drawing by animator Marc Davis.

From a mere twinkling light to a full-fledged personality, Tinker Bell has captured the hearts of generations of fans.

From her beginning as a twinkling light in J. M. Barrie's stage play to her unforgettable performance as the sassy sprite in Walt Disney's *Peter Pan* (1953), and her role as a feisty but loyal friend in *Disney Fairies*, Tinker Bell is one of Disney's most iconic and beloved characters. Her charming looks and fiery personality were created by master animator Marc Davis. With only the silvery sound of tinkling bells as a voice, Davis relied solely on Tink's movements to bring the pretty pixie's personality to life. She flits, flirts, fumes, crosses her arms, stamps her feet, and blushes furiously when angry. Tink proved such a favorite with audiences that she soon came to represent the magic of Disney. She sprinkles her pixie dust in the opening of weekly Disney TV shows, appears at the beginning of Disney DVD releases, and flutters above Disneyland Park during the fireworks shows.

▶ The Pixie Dust Tree, the magical heart of Pixie Hollow, spreads its sheltering branches in this Disney Publishing illustration.

TINK GETS A VOICE

In the early 2000s, plans began to expand Tink's world, and she was given a voice for the first time in *Tinker Bell* (2008), provided by voice actress Mae Whitman. But being able to speak wasn't the only change for Tinker Bell. She was also given a distinctive home, Pixie Hollow in Never Land, and a troupe of fairy friends who each have unique talents, from creating things with light and water to taking care of animals and plants. Tinker Bell, as her name suggests, is a master tinker—a whiz at inventing ingenious gadgets. She is the

◀ Tink and her *Disney Fairies* friends. Clockwise from Tinker Bell: Periwinkle, Rosetta, Iridessa, Silvermist, Fawn, and Vidia.

irrepressible heart of the group in each of the seven films released for home entertainment to date. In *The Secret of the Wings* (2012), we discover that she has a sister, and in *Tinker Bell and the Legend of the NeverBeast* (2015) Tink and her friends worry about a

new furry addition to Pixie Hollow. Impulsive, impatient, and determined, Tinker Bell remains the charming fairy beloved by so many for so long. She may be only 6 in (15 cm) tall, but her big emotions are ones many can relate to.

TEA PARTY CONCEPT ART
Mary Blair's phantasmagorical concept painting—portraying Alice lost at the
head of a table set with a bewildering assortment of tea things—helped make
the Mad Hatter's Tea Party one of the wildest sequences in Disney animation.

Welcome to Wonderland

From the 1930s right through today, the imaginative wellspring of Disney animation has been fed by the inspirational work of concept artists. These inventive illustrators have stimulated ideas, characters, and even entire sequences with their colorful sketches and paintings. The pre-production artwork of influential stylist and designer Mary Blair appealed to Walt Disney and inspirited the story artists on such films as *Cinderella* (1950) and *Peter Pan* (1953). Her exuberant take on the fantastical world of *Alice in Wonderland* was a particularly strong influence on Walt's 1951 adaptation of Lewis Carroll's literary classic. Blair's many artworks—full of contrasting colors and geographic gymnastics—helped form this happily eccentric animated dreamscape.

THE FINISHED SCENE
Walt Disney was adamant that Mary Blair's unique visions be faithfully translated to the screen. The surreal setting of *Alice in Wonderland* was an ideal environment for the artist's idiosyncratic designs, as seen in this beautiful final film frame.

Duo of Dog Delights

Man's best friend is also one of animation's favorite subjects, as seen from the early days of Pluto up through classic films that have followed in his paw prints.

▼ Animators studied real animals to ensure that the title characters in *Lady and the Tramp* were lifelike while imbuing them with recognizable human traits.

The nostalgic animated feature, *Lady and the Tramp* (1955) centers on the charming romance between a pampered pooch and a streetwise mutt. The film marks a series of Disney firsts—the first Disney animated feature with an everyday American setting and the first animated feature to be photographed in the new widescreen format of CinemaScope®. The artists studied real animals to animate the canine cast, and the model dog for Tramp was actually a female stray found by story artist Ed Penner. Alternative names for Tramp that were considered include Homer, Rags, and Bozo, yet it's hard to imagine calling that scamp anything but Tramp nearly 70 years after he bounded onto the screen.

BETTER THAN BARKING

Lady and the Tramp was based on the short story "Happy Dan, the Whistling Dog" by Ward Greene, adapted for feature length in a mutt-ful and musical way. Popular performer Peggy Lee provided the voice of multiple characters and also memorable singing moments to convey the story of these star-crossed canines. The film has proven popular for generation after generation, inspiring an animated sequel and a live-action reimagining.

◄ Lady, Tramp, their brood, and their furry friends add up to an entertaining mix of canine characters.

"Animals have personalities like people and must be studied." WALT DISNEY

▲ Pongo's eyes were typically drawn with just a dark center as seen here, but special close-up shots featured a colored iris added to further express emotion. Another fun fact: Pongo sports 72 spots while Perdita has 68.

SEEING SPOTS

One Hundred and One Dalmatians (1961) is the tale of Pongo and Perdita, the proud Dalmatian parents who rescue 99 puppies from the evil Cruella De Vil. The feature film pioneered the use of the Xerox camera, a timesaving device that eliminated the inking process and transferred the animators' drawings directly to animation cels. Each of the dog's spot patterns were designed like a constellation in order to maintain continuity frame-to-frame. With its sharp angles and thick lines, the art direction incorporated the sketchy Xerox look, giving the film the contemporary style of a sophisticated pen-and-ink drawing. The painting of spots and other color effects required an estimated 800 gallons (about 3,000 litres) of paint, blended into 1,000 custom tones.

ADDED ANIMAL ANTICS

Adapted from the novel *The Hundred and One Dalmatians* by Dodie Smith, the movie was so beloved that it bred multiple follow-up stories in an animated sequel, two animated series, and two live-action films. Cruella's infamous fame led to a live-action fictional biopic, and even the fictional television show that the spotted family watches, *Adventures of Thunderbolt*, has led to a spin-off short.

▼ Story sketch of the Dalmatian clan by Bill Peet. According to Disney publicity, there is a total of 6,469,952 spots on the Dalmatians in 113,760 frames of the final film.

A Rose By Any Other Name

In *Sleeping Beauty*, Disney animation brings the secret princess, with her subtle style and grace, to life.

▲ Actress Helene Stanley portrayed Aurora in live-action reference footage for the animators (left to right: Marc Davis, John Lounsbery, and Milt Kahl).

Cursed at birth by the wicked fairy Maleficent, Princess Aurora is renamed Briar Rose and hidden in the woods by the three good fairies until her 16th birthday. *Sleeping Beauty* (1959) character designer Tom Oreb based Aurora's style on that of artist Eyvind Earle's medieval-inspired backgrounds, using strong vertical lines for both her

▼ Aurora's beautiful singing voice captures the attention of Prince Phillip and the pair instantly fall in love, as seen in this cel setup.

peasant clothes and her pink gown, and he created stylized swirls for her hair. Movie star Audrey Hepburn also provided inspiration for Aurora's elegant poise, and the princess moves with a refined grace, thanks to the talents of animator Marc Davis.

MONUMENTAL MUSIC

The score for *Sleeping Beauty* was a complicated assignment for George Bruns, who was tasked with reworking music from the namesake four-hour

Russian ballet (written by Pyotr Tchaikovsky) to fit into the construct of the film. The classic "Once Upon a Dream" was written by composer Sammy Fain and lyricist Jack Lawrence, and other songs were crafted by Tom Adair, Winston Hibler, and Ted Sears.

SWEET SINGING VOICE

Aurora is given the "gift of song" at birth, so her dulcet voice was an integral part of her personality.

▲ Eyvind Earle portrays the battle between Prince Phillip and Maleficent in this piece of concept art. Maleficent has since won audiences' attention with two live-action films and various television projects about her own progeny.

"From the time I started making motion pictures I dreamed of bringing Sleeping Beauty to life through ... animation." WALT DISNEY

Encouraged by Walt Disney to "paint with her voice," singer Mary Costa helped bring the secret princess's personality to life. Her graceful movements, elegant design, and nuanced emotions make audiences feel as if they, too, have met Aurora in a dream.

ARTISTIC RICHNESS

Sleeping Beauty was an ambitious artistic endeavor by Walt Disney, whose continued desire for innovative filmmaking was no surprise to his crew. In a thoughtful effort to bring the graphic style of artist Eyvind Earle to life, some animation drawings were so complicated that they took up to five hours to craft. In addition, the level of detail and artistic precision needed to produce art for a larger-than-ever wide screen projection from 70mm film made for intensive labor. This all meant that *Sleeping Beauty* was the most expensive animated feature film made as of that point in cinematic history, with an estimated budget of $6 million.

► Eyvind Earle-styled rendition of a storybook ending for *Sleeping Beauty* in this book art glows with medieval charm in romantic pink tones.

A Lasting Hurrah

A swingin' safari of music, fun, and brilliant character animation, *The Jungle Book* would end up being Walt's animated farewell to the world.

Walt had considered Rudyard Kipling's famous collection of stories, with its many lively animal personalities, as an ideal subject for Disney animation since the mid-1930s. He finally bought the screen rights in 1962. However, the great storyteller felt that Kipling's tales were too somber. He assigned the Sherman Brothers to compose some breezy songs—"The Bare Necessities" had already been written by Terry Gilkyson—to help make the film a playful romp, and the brothers created songs in lively styles as disparate as jazz and barber shop. Baloo, the dignified, lawgiving bear of the original book was transformed into a carefree character,

▲ A story sketch rendered in colored pencil of the confrontation between Shere Khan and Kaa.

▶ Bear and boy: Baloo and Mowgli are the center of the film.

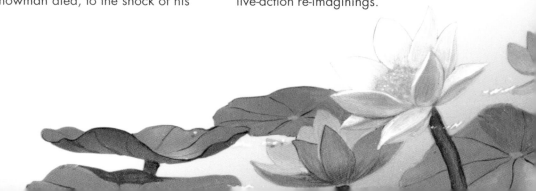

◄ Bagheera discovers a strange creature that turns out to be a man-cub.

"He's with me, ain't he? And I'll learn him all I know." BALOO THE BEAR

and the relationship between him and Mowgli the man-cub became the heart of the film. Walt inspired his team of elite animators by pantomiming Baloo's happy-go-lucky walk for animator Ollie Johnston, and wildly flapping his arms up and down as he acted out the antics of the mop-topped vultures for animator Eric Larson.

THE CHARACTERS ARE THE STORY
Walt sought a fresh approach to villainy for Shere Khan, the film's arrogant antagonist. When character

designer Ken Anderson added an air of superiority to his sketch of the powerful tiger, Walt took one look at this interpretation and knew it was exactly the attitude he was seeking for the movie's chief villain. Directing animator Milt Kahl then drew the contemptuous tiger as a caricature of sophisticated actor George Sanders. From greatly expanding the roles of Baloo and Kaa the sinister serpent, to ordering changes in the design of characters, Walt was, as ever, the creative catalyst.

AFTER WALT
In the midst of production, on December 15, 1966, the great showman died, to the shock of his

longtime creative team. Without Walt, Woolie Reitherman—the first to be given a sole animation director's credit by Walt on *The Sword in the Stone* (1963)—set out to guide the film to completion. Thirty years after the triumph of Walt's first animated feature, *Snow White and the Seven Dwarfs*, *The Jungle Book* premiered at Hollywood's world-famous Grauman's Chinese Theatre on October 18, 1967. The freewheeling new animated feature was an enormous international hit, reaffirming animation as crafted by Walt Disney as an art form for the ages. It also spawned successors including the animated series *Jungle Cubs* and multiple live-action re-imaginings.

Finding the Way After Walt

After Walt's passing, the animation division had to chart a course without their original captain at the helm.

▲ Thomas O'Malley cleans up nicely when welcomed into the refined world of Duchess and her kittens Berlioz, Toulouse, and Marie.

❝ What would Walt do?" was a common question in the minds of filmmakers at the Disney studio after their founder and chief executive of inspiration was longer available to answer this question directly. Not only was Walt's absence felt in the late 1960s, but a few of the Disney chief animation talents—those referred to reverently as the "Nine Old Men"—were also moving into other areas of focus. The first few films in this era represented an interesting time of rediscovery for the studio, sharing stories old and new cast with characters of all animal-kind.

FANCY FELINES

The Aristocats (1970) tells the tale of a posh cat mother and her three kittens who are unexpectedly swiped away from their pampered life, finding themselves stranded in the countryside without a clue what to do. Duchess and her kittens are lucky to meet O'Malley, a kindly street cat who helps them return to Paris, with some fun adventures and other vibrant characters along the way, including old country dogs Napoleon and Lafayette. *The Aristocats* was one of the last films to be green-lit by Walt himself, and the movie is musically enhanced by the delightful tunes of the Sherman Brothers. At various points in the story's development, it was considered as a potential two-part television project, and also a live-action feature. Its ultimate creation as an animated film incorporated over 325,000 drawings that were crafted by 35 animators—played out in 20 sequences that required 1,125 separate scenes and 900 painted backgrounds. Five of the "Nine Old Men" legendary animators worked on *The Aristocats*, and a familiar voice also appears in this film: Phil Harris, who Walt Disney himself had chosen to provide the voice of Baloo in *The Jungle Book*, voiced Thomas O'Malley.

◄ Concept art from *The Aristocats* by Ken Anderson, depicting the good times celebrated in the song "Ev'rybody Wants to Be a Cat."

▲ Maid Marian, Robin Hood, Little John, and a whole band of merry characters share a fun moment of song.

"*You're no outlaw. Why, someday you'll be called a great hero.*"

FRIAR TUCK

AN OLD TALE

Robin Hood (1973) is an animated retelling of the famous legend. The well-known figures, such as Friar Tuck and the Sheriff of Nottingham, are "performed" by a cast of delightfully caricatured animals. The country and western elements of the soundtrack set the film apart from other traditional Disney animated features—as does the tale, which is set in England.

▶ *Robin Hood* concept art by Ken Anderson of the sly fox

Silly Old Bear

Disney animation brings to life the endearing characters and whimsical wisdom of A. A. Milne's original *Winnie the Pooh* books about the bear of very little brain.

▲ Story sketch of Winnie the Pooh with his honey pot

Who's the most lovable bear around? It shouldn't take too much think-think-thinking to come up with the answer: Winnie the Pooh. First introduced to Disney fans in *Winnie the Pooh and the Honey Tree* (1966), the huggable, honey-loving teddy bear and his captivating friends were created by British author A. A. Milne in 1924, inspired by the stuffed toys of his young son, Christopher Robin. As early as 1937, Walt wanted

to animate Milne's witty stories. When he acquired the screen rights in 1961, the great showman sought to retain the delicate whimsy of the literary work. Story artist Bill Justice recalled Walt's specific direction to maintain the charm of the writing and the characters. Walt also wanted his artists to stay true to the spirit and integrity of the pen-and-ink drawings of E. H. Shepard in adapting the visuals to Disney animation. In drawing these quaint characters, Disney designers gave Pooh a thumb so he could pick up objects (mostly honey pots) and Piglet cheeks to make his face more expressive, but they maintained the whimsical appeal and basic design of the originals.

A FILM AND TV STAR

At first, Walt envisioned *Winnie the Pooh* as a feature, but as the story developed he decided to produce shorter featurettes to be followed by a feature film. *Winnie the Pooh and the Blustery Day* (1968), which introduced both Piglet and Tigger, was developed at the same time as *Winnie the Pooh and the Honey Tree*. When it was released, it won an Academy Award® as Best Short Subject – Cartoons. These first featurettes were combined with the Oscar®-nominated *Winnie the Pooh and Tigger Too* (1974) to become the feature-length *The Many Adventures of Winnie the Pooh* (1977). The cuddly bear became a TV star in 1988 with *The Many Adventures of Winnie the Pooh*, which won two Daytime Emmy® Awards for Best Animated Program and was followed by other series and specials. *The Tigger Movie* (2000) led to more features, including *Piglet's Big Movie* (2003), *Winnie the Pooh* (2011), and the hybrid live-action/animated film *Christopher Robin* (2018).

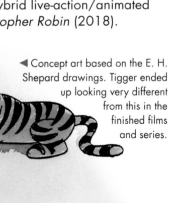

◀ Concept art based on the E. H. Shepard drawings. Tigger ended up looking very different from this in the finished films and series.

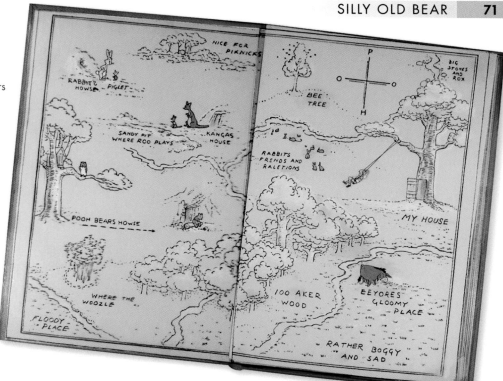

► The featurettes opened with a Hundred Acre Wood map based on the endpapers drawn by E. H. Shepard.

◄ Animation drawing of Tigger by Milt Kahl

"*The beauty is in the tenderness and warmth of the characters.*" WOOLIE REITHERMAN (ANIMATION DIRECTOR)

▼ Production background painting of the Hundred Acre Wood

▲ The legendary animation talent shown here includes (front row, l–r) Woolie Reitherman, Les Clark, Ward Kimball, and John Lounsbery; (back row, l–r) Milt Kahl, Marc Davis, Frank Thomas, Eric Larson, and Ollie Johnston.

Passing the Pencils Along

As the last of the "Nine Old Men" retired in the 1980s, their legacy was handed off to a new generation of animators to continue in the Disney artistic tradition. The variety of feature films from this timeframe would usher in new fans for generations to come.

The Fox and the Hound (1981) was the 24th Disney animated feature film, telling the story of two unlikely animal friends: a red fox named Tod and a hound dog named Copper. It was the last film that dynamic animating duo Frank Thomas and Ollie Johnston worked on together, with Woolie Reitherman co-producing, and Eric Larson acting as a consultant. This was the first Disney film on which future animation legends including Brad Bird, Tim Burton, and John Musker worked, alongside a whole crew of notable names to come. The popularity of this adventure led to the creation of The Fox and the Hound 2 in 2006.

▶ Young fox Tod and hound Copper frolic in the forest as depicted in concept art by Mel Shaw.

MAGIC AND MAYHEM

The Black Cauldron (1985) was the first Disney animated film to receive a PG rating, and also the first to be heard through the Dolby sound system. Decades later, fans continue to debate what type of creature Gurgi is, while the film quietly takes its place in Disney history as the first animated feature to include computer-generated imagery—bringing the very cauldron for which the movie is named into existence.

CAT-CHY TUNES

Oliver & Company (1988), the 27th feature from Walt Disney Animation Studios, follows the story of an orphaned Oliver resonant of the Charles Dickens character—but this tale stars a feline protagonist and a pop music soundtrack including the vocal stylings of popular 1980s artists Billy Joel, Huey Lewis, Bette Midler, and Ruth Pointer. Another musical note of interest: *Oliver & Company* was the first instance that famed Broadway talent Howard Ashman wrote lyrics for a Disney film.

▲ Concept art by Mel Shaw portrays Tod and Copper in their later years, reflecting on their friendship and lives.

▼ A character size comparison chart shows how Oliver and his canine friends measure up to one another.

Making a Splash

The story of a princess who is fascinated by the human world, *The Little Mermaid* ushered in a renaissance of Disney animation.

▲ Ariel's youthful spirit shines through in this colored pencil character sketch by Glen Keane.

The first new Disney princess to appear on screen since Princess Aurora in Walt Disney's *Sleeping Beauty* (1959), Ariel in *The Little Mermaid* (1989) is different from her three predecessors. Not only is she not human, the lively mermaid is a curious, rebellious teenager who dreams of completely transforming herself and leaving the world she lives in behind. When she rescues Prince Eric from the sea, Ariel's wish to be with him becomes one of the influences that drives her to act upon her dreams.

LONG TIME COMING

The development of an animated version of the Hans Christian Andersen fairy tale was initiated at Disney in the 1930s but then set aside, only to be rediscovered in the archives some 50 years later when the concept was finally given a green light. The popularity of *The Little Mermaid* inspired a ripple of further works including a home entertainment sequel and prequel, a Broadway production, a live television broadcast, theme park attractions, and a live-action film.

▼ Light-filled color in this concept art by Andy Gaskill helped influence the Caribbean-inspired palette for *The Little Mermaid*.

◀ Sebastian and his finned friends sing the praises of ocean life in the song "Under the Sea."

"What makes Ariel real and identifiable is her struggle to be free and her father's struggle to let her grow up." GLEN KEANE (ANIMATOR)

CURIOUS CHARACTERISTICS

Ariel's youthful voice (provided by Jodi Benson) is both a charm to audiences and an appealing gift that the evil sea witch Ursula cannot wait to get her tentacles and vocal chords wrapped around. Meanwhile, Ariel's hair gave Disney animators a creative challenge, which was portraying a believable and manageable style while being submerged in most scenes. To create the hair's flowing movement underwater, animators studied footage of astronaut Sally Ride when she was in space. Yet perhaps the most standout characteristic for Ariel is her courage as she risks everything to determine her own life—paving the way for a whole new era of self-empowered princesses.

◀ Ursula appears to be crooning malevolently in this color model image by Disney Studio Artists.

BIGGER AND BADDER

Ursula, the villain with many tentacles and theatrical gestures, gained a grander role on screen than the sea witch character had in the original fairy tale. Early development of her role in the movie suggested that she might be Triton's sister and thus Ariel's aunt. The final film version of an independent Ursula has proven to be an audience favorite with her intimidating yet comedic demeanor. The vocal talents of Pat Carroll brought Ursula to life in a bewitching and booming blend of swagger and song.

AN OCEAN OF SONG

The Little Mermaid was a breakout collaboration for the musical writing team of composer Alan Menken and lyricist Howard Ashman. Their work was honored with two Academy Awards®—"Best Original Score" and "Best Original Song" for "Under the Sea."

Booksmart Over Brawn

A reader and a dreamer, Belle seeks adventure as the heroine in her own story.

▲ A tentative attraction grows between the two dancers, portrayed in this graphite concept sketch by Glen Keane.

Belle's intelligence, compassion, and sincerity are the driving force in *Beauty and the Beast* (1991)—a timeless tale of love's redemptive power. Belle dreams of adventure outside the provincial town where she lives with her father and discovers more than her share of it when she encounters the Beast and those who reside with him in the magical but somewhat menacing castle environment.

▲ Bookworm Belle navigates the streets of her town.

▶ Gaston is proud to show off his strength.

BRIGHT BEAUTY

Belle's love of reading sets her apart from the other villagers, a fact that the Disney artists visually reinforced in the film's opening scene by making her the only character dressed in blue. Despite her dreaminess, Belle is also practical and down to earth. Her relaxed, natural good looks were inspired by actress and singer Judy Garland, and animators chose actress Paige O'Hara to be the voice of Belle because it reminded them of Judy Garland's rich, warm tones. Belle doesn't seem to notice how beautiful she is—for her, it is the person within that counts. It isn't her beauty that affects and changes the Beast's heart, but her kindness, patience, and sympathy. While Belle is teaching him etiquette and how to read, she is also teaching him how to love. At the same time, Belle learns to look beyond a harsh exterior to see the humanity and kindness buried within the beastly creature—a lesson that ties into her passion for literature by proving "you can't judge a book by its cover."

▶ A cast of utensils and dishware come-to-life serve up the lively "Be Our Guest" song.

AN ILLUSTRATION OF LOVE

The traditionally animated *Beauty and the Beast* was introduced to its public in a rather non-traditional way: it premiered as a "work in progress" at the 1991 New York Film Festival, with nearly a third of the rough edit containing scenes still in storyboard and animation test phases. Apparently its unique debut was the start of a path of success: *Beauty and the Beast* was the first animated film to win a Golden Globe Award for "Best Motion Picture, Musical or Comedy" and also the first animated feature film to be nominated for the Academy Award® for "Best Motion Picture."

▶ A storyboard sketch by Chris Sanders conjures the magic of love.

MOVED BY MUSIC

Musical storytelling magic was conjured once again by the writing team of composer Alan Menken and lyricist Howard Ashman. The song "Beauty and the Beast" won both a Golden Globe and an Academy Award® for "Best Original Song," and the pop version recorded by Celine Dion and Peabo Bryson also won two Grammy Awards.

THE MAGIC CONTINUES

Audiences have enjoyed a number of other pieces inspired by the animated film, including a long-running Broadway show, an IMAX reissue that included the song "Human Again," multiple home entertainment sequels, a live-action film, and a television special celebrating its 30th anniversary.

▼ Evoking the stained glass art at the film's beginning, this concept art by Brian McEntee, Mac George, and Vance Gerry completes the story.

"The lessons of the Beauty and the Beast story are truly timeless: you can't judge a book by its cover, and beauty is only skin deep."

LINDA WOOLVERTON (SCREENWRITER)

Some of the most beloved characters from *Beauty and the Beast* are the magical inhabitants of the Beast's castle, including Mrs. Potts, Lumiere, and Cogsworth. The animators faced a challenge in creating motion and personality for household objects, so they focused on an impression of movement and a wide variety of facial expressions. As a result, they were able to make everyday objects truly come to life! The castle dwellers are essential to guiding the audience through the story, and they add warmth and humor to an otherwise dark tale.

A Whole New World

Like a gleaming treasure uncovered in the Cave of Wonders, *Aladdin* glows with a jewel-like color palette and a signature style uniquely its own.

▲ Genie drawing by Eric Goldberg. The graceful, curvy lines of legendary caricaturist Al Hirschfeld influenced the designs of all the characters.

Weaving a tapestry of romance, adventure, and enchantment, *Aladdin* (1992) is an animated adaptation of the Arabian Nights tale of a lad and his magic lamp. In the fabled city of Agrabah, a young "diamond in the rough" teams up with an outrageous shape-shifting Genie to win the heart of Princess Jasmine while trying to outsmart the wicked vizier Jafar.

COLORS ARE KEY

In a production where color and shape defined personalities, the design team set out to create a unity of character and environment and used a vivid color palette with a level of saturation reminiscent of Disney's early animated classics. The artists went to great lengths to create the film's signature style. Artistic supervisor for the layout

▶ According to background director, Kathy Altieri, the colors and design of the backgrounds affect the audience's emotions. This background painting of the Sultan's palace at sunset has a red hue, which indicates a future bad turn of events for Aladdin and Jasmine.

001 01.1 002 02.1 04.1 005 07.2 008 08.1 009

▲ This color script was developed by production designer Richard Vander Wende to map out the emotional impact of colors throughout *Aladdin*, sequence by sequence.

department and Iranian Rasoul Azadani returned to his hometown of Isfahan to photograph more than 1800 shots to assist the artists in creating the design of Agrabah. Production designer Richard Vander Wende turned to ancient Persian miniatures, incorporating many of their design elements, such as their vibrant colors, into the film. Background director Kathy Altieri explained that since blue is associated with water, a life-giving force in the desert, the film's heroes are depicted in the cooler range of colors while villains are in the red range. This can be seen in the true-blue Genie and the red-and-black clad Jafar.

SHAPING THE CHARACTERS
Vander Wende had the *Aladdin* artists use the thick and thin 'S' curve seen in Arabic calligraphy. The designs are based on caricatured drawings that emphasize these curves and shapes, where one shape organically leads into another. This fluid caricature style was even worked into the animation itself, particularly with the Genie. Art director Bill Perkins emphasized the shape relationships of the main characters and the interior/exterior locations that would best fit their personalities. Aladdin's wide stance, narrow waist, and broad shoulders are visually distinct from Jafar's sharp-edged T-shape, which in turn contrasts with the Genie, referred to by Perkins as an anti-gravity machine because of his floating mass which tapers down to nothing. The Sultan's throne room reflects his rounded shape with an egg motif seen in the columns, throne, and oil lamps. When Jafar gains control of the kingdom, the shapes in the Sultan's room transform to echo the pointed silhouette of the scheming sorcerer.

A WHOLE NEW KIND OF HEROINE
Jasmine's attitude and confidence were illustrated by Disney supervising animator Mark Henn. Henn looked at a number of live models before he realized his inspiration was right in front of him—in the form of a graduation photo of his younger sister Beth. It was then that Jasmine became a reality. She is a brave young woman with a mind of her own—and the courage to jump over any wall and discover life on her own terms.

◀ A clean-up animation drawing from a scene animated by Mark Henn conveys the excitement and romance of Aladdin and Jasmine's exhilarating magic carpet ride.

▲ Color Key of Young Simba and Mufasa looking out over the Pride Lands.

Animals Rule

In the great tradition of animated Disney animal tales, *The Lion King* explores universal truths about honoring heritage and living responsibly and became a worldwide phenomenon.

The Lion King (1994) boldly tells the epic tale of a lion cub named Simba and his journey of self-discovery as he follows in the paw prints of his father, the great king Mufasa. An enormous international hit that also inspired a popular stage version, this musical animal allegory celebrates the "circle of life."

EPIC INSPIRATION

The earliest version of the Serengeti-set story, originally entitled *King of the Jungle*, came about in 1989 when the idea of creating an animated feature about lions was first considered. The story was inspired in part by allegories and spiritual stories, such as the accounts of Joseph and Moses of the Old Testament. With its themes of responsibility and maturation, the filmmakers felt there was a certain religious epic quality to this coming-of-age tale.

▼ Color study for the opening "Circle of Life" sequence depicts the color palette for the movie.

"The Lion King is essentially a love story between a father and a son." DON HAHN (PRODUCER)

▶ Story sketch by Burny Mattinson of Simba and his wastrel pals Timon and Pumbaa

GOING ON SAFARI

Real lions, including a cub, two young adults, and a fully-grown male and female were brought to the Disney Studios for the animators to study. In November 1991, six of the filmmakers embarked on a two-week artistic safari to Kenya in North Africa. With cameras and sketchbooks, the artists journeyed across the African savanna by Land Rover™, seeing lions and hyenas up close. The artists' safari guides tied a rope to their vehicle and drove slowly as lion cubs chased after the rope, playing with it like house cats. The artists photographed scenery to help them capture an authentic African savanna in their art, including an entire rainstorm moving across the plains.

MUSICAL MASTERPIECE

With a powerful Academy Award®-winning score by Hans Zimmer, the film features songs written by Sirs Elton John and Tim Rice. "Can You Feel the Love Tonight" won the Oscar® for Best Original Song in 1994. "Circle of Life" and "Hakuna Matata" were also nominated in the same Academy Award® category. The most successful film of 1994, *The Lion King* was the highest-grossing animated feature ever produced up until that time, and the Broadway show that it inspired has become the top-earning production in box office history, as of its 25th year anniversary. Fans have enjoyed a number of subsequent inspired projects based on *The Lion King*, including two home entertainment sequels, two television series, and a CG reimagining in 2019.

▲ A fully grown Simba and Nala from the "Can You Feel the Love Tonight" sequence

The Lion King's opening scene is one of the most memorable in the history of cinema, both visually and musically. The sequence originally included dialogue, but when directors Roger Allers and Rob Minkoff heard the final version of "Circle of Life," they decided that words were no longer needed. The combination of this powerful song, beautiful animation, and the introduction of an important young lion cub draws viewers into the story before the opening credits of the movie are even shown.

Connected to Nature

Pocahontas was the first Disney princess to be based on a real person.

▲ Meeko and Flit, the furred and feathered forest companions of Pocahontas, were brought to life through the animation of Nik Ranieri and Dave Pruiksma.

Pocahontas (1995) is inspired by the story of the historical figure known as Pocahontas, who lived more than 400 years ago and was a member of the Powhatan people. The real Pocahontas was younger than Disney's character when she encountered John Smith, and "Pocahontas" was actually a nickname—her given name was Amonute, and she was also known as Matoaka.

◄ Photographic reproduction of watercolor concept art depicting Pocahontas and "colors of the wind."

▲ The majestic beauty of nature is employed via stunning vistas in *Pocahontas*.

STRONG AND COURAGEOUS

Disney artists saw Pocahontas as a young, curious, and intrepid woman trying to bridge two different worlds and find her own path between them. Animated by Glen Keane and voiced by Iñupiaq and Métis Irene Bedard, Pocahontas exudes confidence and athleticism. One of the strongest Disney princesses, both physically and spiritually, she is a complex character—brave, daring, and compassionate, with a deep spiritual connection to nature. In *Pocahontas*, Disney created a heroine whose heart is truly painted with all the colors of the wind.

SONGS FROM THE HEART OF THE WOODS

While stunning visuals portray the beauty of the landscape, music provides a rich audial experience as the soundtrack to the adventure. Songs by Pocahontas are conveyed through the singing voice of Broadway star Judy Kuhn, as written by composer Alan Menken and lyricist Stephen Schwartz who together researched the history of Jamestown, Virginia. Their musical efforts were honored with two Academy Awards®—"Best Original Score" and "Best Original Song" for "Colors of the Wind."

▶ Disney hosted a record-breaking film premiere event for *Pocahontas*, drawing an audience of over 100,000 people to watch a live show, screening, and fireworks display in New York City's Central Park on June 10, 1995.

Life in the Bell Tower

The 34th Disney animated feature rang true for audiences who enjoyed a tale of drama and song about an otherwise unsung hero.

▲ Concept art of Quasimodo rescuing Esmeralda by Peter DeSeve.

▼ Gargoyles Hugo, Victor, and Laverne add color commentary from on high in this concept art by Kathy Zielinski and Lisa Keene.

Inspired by the classic story written by Victor Hugo, Disney's *The Hunchback of Notre Dame* (1996) was set upon a musical foundation hewn by the songwriting team of Alan Menken and Steven Schwartz. Artists in Disney studio facilities in Florida, Burbank, and Paris collaborated to animate the epic tale of Quasimodo, Esmeralda, Phoebus, and an ever-endearing trio of Gargoyles, whose friendship with Quasimodo could turn the coldest stone into a bundle of heartwarming love.

MEDIEVAL YET MODERN

Disney artists sought to create a cinematic world that channeled Hugo's own Gothic illustrations and interpreted his three-tiered universe into their versions of Heaven (the skies) and Hell (the streets of Paris) with the bell tower serving as a bridge in between the two extremes. The technology team contributed to rounding out the theatrical experience by providing an innovative technique for crowd animation.

The heroic rope-swinging and belfry-climbing actions of Quasimodo required boundary-pushing camera work to bring audiences along for his highly mobile, often vertical and airborne, adventures. Quasimodo's connection with audiences rang so true that Disney delivered a live stage musical of his story in 1999 and has also been developing a live-action feature to bring his story into even greater reality.

◄ Story sketch of Quasimodo in the cathedral by Kelly Wightman

Zero to Hero

Disney's demigod celebrity lit up the big screen with Mount Olympus-sized song and fanfare.

The Greco-Roman legend of Hercules was a perfect character to portray as an animated superhero—bigger than life but still relatable because he is half human. For Disney's *Hercules* (1997), filmmakers chose the Roman interpretation of his name since it is more widely recognized in modern culture, but leaned toward Greek inspiration in other character elements and architecture, as well as the overall style, which was crafted by production designer Gerald Scarfe.

> *"He has a power, a sweep to his lines, an incredible energy and vitality, to which we gave a Disney translation."*

ALICE DEWEY (PRODUCER), ON GERALD SCARFE

▲ Concept art of Hercules riding Pegasus by Gerald Scarfe.

▼ Hades is all fired up, as shown in this concept art by Gerald Scarfe.

CELESTIAL SIGHTS AND SOUNDS

Beyond the cast of stylized gods and goddesses, audiences were treated to a technical wonder in the form of the Hydra, a thirty-headed beast of Hades, brought to computer-generated screen life by a talented team of artists and animators. The Muses musically narrated the epic tale of Hercules through songs crafted by composer Alan Menken and lyricist David Zippel. The music writing team regrouped to launch the live theater version *Hercules* that debuted in 2019, and a revised version of the show returned to stages in 2023. An animated peek back into Hercules's history played out in a 1998 television series about his time at the Prometheus Academy, and in the home entertainment prequel *Hercules: Zero to Hero* (1999).

Family Honor

Inspired by a Chinese legend, Mulan's story makes her a unique Disney heroine.

Disney's first animated feature set in China, *Mulan* (1998) features a young woman who poses as a male warrior and secretly takes her father's place in the Imperial Army, leaving home to undergo combat training. Supervising animator Mark Henn found this brave heroine a challenge, as he was animating not only Mulan but also her soldier persona Ping—two very distinct personalities. Henn was also tasked with the fact that Mulan has more costume changes than any Disney heroine before her. With the help of character and costume designer Chen-Yi Chang, they created a character whose design is rooted in traditional Chinese artwork wherein linework is not overdrawn, but more about implying than showing detail, thus bringing to life the figure found in many versions of Chinese folklore. Mulan's costume base color is green to reflect her connection with nature and her desire to be outdoors, even when she is supposed to stay at home.

▲ Delicate pen and marker story sketch by Chris Sanders and Joe Mateo conveys Mulan's awe and respect for her father, Fa Zhou.

FINDING HER PLACE

Whatever her guise, Mulan's driving force is her desire to bring honor to her family, while ultimately remaining true to herself. Mulan eventually discovers courage within, but it is not until she drops her disguise and acts like her true self that she really triumphs.

"Mulan doesn't accept that she's powerless. That's what makes her great." PAM COATS (PRODUCER)

◄ Mulan is torn by who she is expected to be, and who she believes she should be, as she ponders in the song "Reflection."

▶ Mulan transforms herself into Ping to cover her family's military duty in order to save her elderly father from service.

YIN AND YANG

The emotional Mushu and the rational Cri-Kee are both important companions on Mulan's journey. Mushu conveys a classic Chinese-style serpentine shape as a dragon, and, as a cricket, Cri-Kee represents a symbol of good luck in Chinese culture. Together they remain true to Mulan, respecting and believing in her authentic self, even when Mulan herself has momentary doubts about rising to the challenge she faces.

▲ The beauty of the Chinese landscape and Mulan's bold spirit are evoked in concept art by Ric Sluiter.

▼ General Li and his troops set forth against a mountainous backdrop inspired by the city of Guilin in China.

▼ Demoted family guardian spirit Mushu and his sidekick Cri-Kee in a story sketch by Floyd Norman

Dinos, Duos, and a Deep Dive

The locations and time continuums were widespread in the animated filmscapes Disney crafted at the turn of the 21st century.

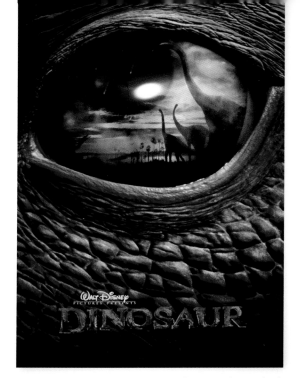

▲ Disney's *Dinosaur* brings audiences back in time to explore prehistoric days on planet Earth, as envisioned through a much more modern animation medium.

In a span of just a few years, Disney animation ran the gamut from traditional 2D animation to groundbreaking CG films, and ranged from storytelling inspired by classic tales and original prehistoric dramas, to buddy comedies and exciting science-fiction adventures.

EONS AGO

Dinosaur (2000) was not only the tender story of a young *Iguanodon* named Aladar, but also the only feature film created in-house at Walt Disney Feature Animation through an innovative visual effects studio called "The Secret Lab." A combination of computer-generated characters and breathtakingly beautiful live-action backgrounds brought audiences back in time via extremely modern technology. Composer James Newton Howard crafted the score, his first animated project for Disney, and audiences were also treated to the vocal stylings of Lebo M, whose prior presence in *The Lion King* was a performance of epic proportions in itself.

◄ Aladar and other creatures seek to escape a treacherous Earth-bound meteor shower in *Dinosaur*.

BOOM BABY

The Emperor's New Groove (2000) casts a spell of fun and fantasy set during the times of the Incan Empire and features the first human-turned-llama character in animated Disney history. The unexpected and humorous duo of on-screen pairings Kuzco and Pacha, and Kronk and Yzma, gained an energetic fan base that inspired further adventures in both the home entertainment sequel *Kronk's New Groove* (2005) and an animated series, *The Emperor's New School* (2006). Bucky the Squirrel has also enjoyed quite the squeakity-squeaking following.

▲ Yzma and Kronk are more of a comical than a criminal pairing, but they do mix up a bit of trouble and a mean batch of spinach puffs, collectively speaking.

▲ Human Kuzco sports a large ego, which ultimately leads to a critical change in his life, courtesy of Yzma.

UNDER THE SEA

The dark depths of the ocean are the setting for the action-packed animated adventure *Atlantis: The Lost Empire* (2001). Comic-book creator Mike Mignola brought his artistic touch to the film, James Newton Howard provided another sweeping soundtrack, and the production team even commissioned the development of an Atlantean language to create a richer, otherworldly experience. The dedicated *Atlantis* fan base has continued to remain strong decades after the premiere, and audiences have been able to follow more of the story through the home entertainment sequel, *Milo's Return* (2003).

▲ The submarine *Ulysses* is caught in the grips of a formidable floating fiend in *Atlantis: The Lost Empire*.

▶ Milo, Princess Kida, and Obby explore the deep dark sea in *Milo's Return*.

▲ Traditional watercolor background
of Lilo's Hawai'i home by Peter Moehrle

Watercolor to Anime

Mischievous alien Stitch zaps through animation styles, from the classic watercolor look of Walt's films to cutting-edge anime.

Writer/director Chris Sanders first sketched a monstrous character who lived in an isolated forest 17 years before *Lilo & Stitch* (2002) was released. Those sketches went on to inspire the offbeat animated film about a pugnacious planet-hopping alien known as Experiment 626 and the lonely Hawaiian girl who befriends the creature and names him Stitch. As Sanders' idea evolved, rather than the usual storyboards animators tend to employ, he created a 15-page book with watercolor illustrations. Seeing this storybook-like presentation, fellow writer/director Dean DeBlois was especially taken with Lilo's quirky but loving personality and the way she and Stitch unexpectedly affect each other's lives.

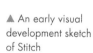

▲ An early visual development sketch of Stitch

REVIVING TRADITIONS

Originally Sanders had thought of sparsely populated Kansas for Stitch's touchdown point, but while planning a trip to Hawai'i, he realized that the islands, surrounded by thousands of miles of water, would be the perfect setting. Production designer Paul Felix and art director Ric Sluiter believed that Sanders' loose, translucent watercolors were the perfect medium for capturing

▼ Concept sketch of Stitch guzzling food.

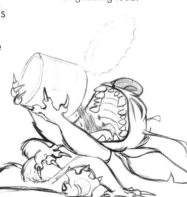

► Advice by hula dancers ensured that Lilo's steps were authentic. Background painting by Ron DeFelice.

▲ ▼ Concept art of cheeky Stitch in action

▲ Stitch and Yuna with friends and foes, clockwise from top left: Hamsterviel, Delia, Takumi, Reika, Toyoda-San, Jumba, Pleakley, BooGoo

the islands' lush landscape and luminous light. Watercolor had not been used for animated backgrounds at Disney since *Bambi*, six decades before, so background supervisor Bob Stanton and his team of 15 painters studied original watercolor backgrounds at the Animation Research Library and trained for six months to learn how to revive the art form for a Disney animated feature.

A MOVIE WITH HEART

Lilo & Stitch echoes *Dumbo*, too, in an important way—the simplicity and warmth of the story. Early on, Sanders and DeBlois decided to focus on developing the characters and their relationships. As Sanders learned more about the rich Hawaiian culture, including the important Hawaiian concept of 'ohana, (family), it became the heart of the film. It is Lilo's strong attachment to her 'ohana that redeems Stitch from his previous destructive programming and gives him the one thing he wasn't designed to have—a family.

ANIME ANTICS

The mischievous blue alien and his adopted Earth family were so loved that *Lilo & Stitch* inspired a television series, *Lilo & Stitch: The Series*, in 2003 and three direct-to-video sequels. Stitch's monstrous popularity in Japan inspired a TV series designed in anime style, *Stitch!* (*Sutitichi!*), taking Experiment 626 to a fictional island off the coast of Okinawa where he shares wild adventures with Yuna, a karate-kicking 10-year-old. *Stitch!* (*Sutitichi!*) aired in Japan from 2008 to 2012, and has since taken the world by storm, Stitch-style.

▲ Young Jim Hawkins in the crow's nest, in concept art by John Ripa

Pirates and Bovines and Bears, Oh My!

From the farthest reaches of the universe to the prairie and the tundra, Disney takes audiences on a range of guided adventures only possible through the magic of animation.

Dynamic directing duo Ron Clements and John Musker took their creativity into deep space with a new Disney interpretation of Robert Louis Stevenson's *Treasure Island*. The animated science-fiction adventure *Treasure Planet* (2002) follows the journey of Jim Hawkins and crew as they search the galaxies for camaraderie and hidden fortune. The film premiered in both traditional and super-screen IMAX format simultaneously to allow audiences the opportunity to scale up their theatrical experience.

GRIZZLED GROWTH

Brother Bear (2003) follows the story of Kenai, whose expedition based on revenge becomes a life-changing and literally form-changing experience. Audiences not only follow his emotional path, but also come to

appreciate Kenai's transformation from a visual perspective—when Kenai is magically transformed into a bear, the cinematic view widens to a broader, more colorful theatrical adventure for the human viewers as well. The final film to be crafted primarily in the Florida-based Disney animation studio, *Brother Bear* leaves a lasting impression with its thoughtful tale of humanity, nature, and the Great Spirits.

▼ An animation drawing of Koda by Sarah Mercey. Koda is the young grizzly companion for Kenai, and their relationship proves to be deeply interwoven in *Brother Bear*.

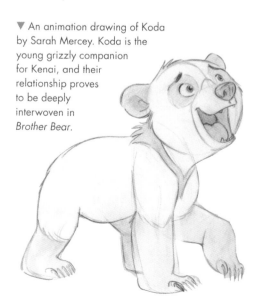

◄ A traditional painting look of cyborg pirate John Silver and young Jim Hawkins represents the blend of classic and modern in Disney's *Treasure Planet*, shown in concept art by Dan Cooper.

▼ Concept art by Richie Chavez portrays some of the key elements in *Brother Bear*.

▶ Rough model sheet for Kenai as created by *Brother Bear* director Aaron Blaise.

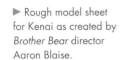

▲ Story sketch by Mark Walton of Lucky Jack and the featured trio of determined cows putting their heads together to solve the farm dilemma in *Home on the Range*.

◀ Concept art of MOO-sical cows in *Home on the Range*

COW POWER

A mighty moo-ing trio of Maggie, Grace, and Mrs. Caloway rally to save their farm in the Western-themed tale, *Home on the Range* (2004). Set to a country soundtrack crafted by Alan Menken and Glenn Slater, and sung by renowned artists such as k.d. lang, Tim McGraw, and Bonnie Raitt, the bovine-turned-bounty hunter story shares a view of the Old West from the perspective of the cow rather than the cowboy.

A New Artistic Dimension

Pushing entertainment and animation boundaries at the same time, Disney produced its first few in-house fully computer-generated animated features in the early 2000s.

▲ *Chicken Little* was not only the first fully computer-animated movie made in-house at Disney, but also premiered a new digital 3D cinematic experience in 100 theaters.

While technology teams worked to build a completely computer-generated animation pipeline (workflow), the artistic team simultaneously worked to create Disney's first ever fully CG animated film, *Chicken Little* (2005). This snappy take on the classic Henny Penny story took a turn into new realms, complete with aliens, baseball, and a karaoke performance of a Spice Girls hit song. It's also a touching story about father Buck Cluck and his son, Chicken Little, who come to understand each other better after experiencing challenges that are bigger and higher than they've ever faced before.

▲ Fish, Abby, Runt, and Chicken Little can't believe what they are seeing in the skies over Oakey Oaks.

◄ Fish, who only speaks in bubbles, tests out the piece of the sky that has fallen as his friends watch in shock and awe.

The small town of Oakey Oaks literally did not know what hit it when pieces of the sky appear to be falling, but the friendly four-pack of misfits Chicken Little, Runt of the Litter, Abby Mallard (the Ugly Duckling), and Fish Out of Water are determined to find out the truth and save all of their own reputations in the process.

KEEP MOVING FORWARD

Inspired in both story and style by William Joyce's *A Day with Wilbur Robinson*, this time-traveling adventure puts young inventor Lewis on a crash course with curious villain Bowler Hat Guy. Luckily, Wilbur Robinson and his unique family come in with an assist that changes the course of history. *Meet the Robinsons* (2007) provides both a heartwarming look at the importance of belonging, and a joyful reminder of Walt Disney's own adage to "keep moving forward."

▲ Lewis discovers that the Robinson family is chock-full of inventive characters and actual inventions, thanks to Wilbur's forward-thinking in *Meet the Robinsons*.

"Not only was 'Keep Moving Forward' the motto for Robinson industries...it's something that I hope the audience will take to heart, especially kids, to help them stay motivated, no matter what challenges life may present." STEPHEN ANDERSON (DIRECTOR)

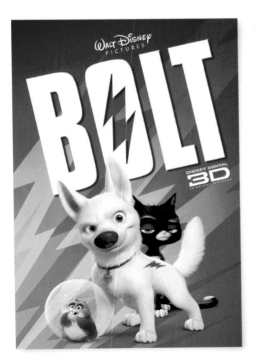

▲ Bolt's design was loosely inspired by the American White Shepherd dog breed, but modified for super-powered cuteness in typical Disney style.

CANINE CHAMPION

It's "ruff" when prized performing pup Bolt takes himself so seriously that he truly believes himself to be the very superhero he plays on film—only to discover that when he needs serious help, he's not that superhero after all. Luckily, the titular character of *Bolt* (2008) collects a duo of friends in the form of alley cat Mittens and hamster Rhino, who help him find his way back cross-country to his Hollywood home. Rhino was truly a homegrown character, as a real-life hamster named Doink was adopted into residency at the studio in Burbank for motion study, and Rhino's voice was cast to Disney story artist Mark Walton.

▶ Bolt, Mittens, and Rhino are a small but fur-midible team in *Bolt*.

Recipe for a Perfect Princess

Disney artists hopped at the chance to create *The Princess and the Frog* in traditional hand-drawn animation.

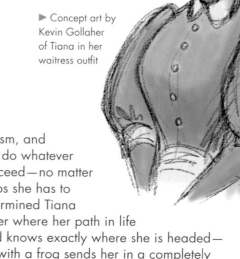

► Concept art by Kevin Gollaher of Tiana in her waitress outfit

The Princess and the Frog (2009) stars Disney's first African-American princess. It was also the first hand-drawn feature film from Walt Disney Animation Studios since 2004, and was a return to the traditional musical—this time with a jazz soundtrack. Practical and realistic, the heroine Tiana doesn't believe in wishing on stars—she is all about working hard to make her dreams come true. Tiana's warmth and beauty come from her humor, optimism, and willingness to do whatever it takes to succeed—no matter how many jobs she has to balance. Determined Tiana doesn't wonder where her path in life is leading and knows exactly where she is headed—until one kiss with a frog sends her in a completely different direction, much to her chagrin.

FOOD FOR THE SOUL

While versions of a film inspired by "The Frog Prince" fairy tale had been in development multiple times in the history of Disney animation, it wasn't until the dynamic directing duo of Ron Clements and John Musker helmed the story of Tiana that the movie finally found its launching (lily)pad. The creative storyline that follows Tiana in her dreams of opening a restaurant in New Orleans to honor her father also draws upon the concept that food brings people together, adding emotional depth to Tiana's story.

"This is it! I'm getting my restaurant!" TIANA

◄ Concept art by Bill Schwab and John Musker of Tiana and Naveen's bayou wedding

◀ The twilight sky glows with light from the Floating Lanterns in this ethereal concept painting by Jeffrey Turley.

"We wanted Rapunzel to be a role model ... and her girl power to drive the story."

BYRON HOWARD (DIRECTOR)

A Golden Adventure

The princess with the flowing locks goes on a journey of discovery, with a little help from the Floating Lanterns.

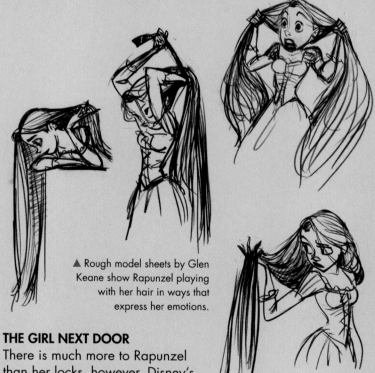

▲ Rough model sheets by Glen Keane show Rapunzel playing with her hair in ways that express her emotions.

Like Sleeping Beauty, Rapunzel from *Tangled* (2010) has no idea she is a princess. She just wants to leave the tower she is locked in to go see the Floating Lanterns. Disney's first computer-generated princess is a self-sufficient young woman who has learned to entertain herself within the confines of the tower walls. She bakes, reads, cleans, exercises, and paints. She also spends a lot of time maintaining her hair—all 70 ft (21 m) of it. Creating Rapunzel's hair was a challenge for the Disney animators—it took three years and the formation of a new software program to animate, resulting in a magical mane that almost appears to have a personality of its own.

THE GIRL NEXT DOOR

There is much more to Rapunzel than her locks, however. Disney's animators wanted the naturally happy young woman to appear down-to-earth and radiate a girl-next-door appeal, which they achieved with the help of voice artist Mandy Moore. Rapunzel may be naïve, but she is also smart, resourceful, and brave enough to leave the tower. When she does, she finds her parents, true love—and herself. Rapunzel's story captivated audiences to follow her into the sequel Disney Channel film *Tangled: Before Ever After* and the series *Rapunzel's Tangled Adventure*.

With a deep scowl, Maximus—the horse of the captain of the guards—grudgingly strikes a truce with Flynn under the encouragement of Rapunzel. Determined Maximus excels at his quest to track down wanted thief Flynn and the makers of *Tangled* were keen to portray the character as a true obstacle to Flynn's success. With his strong neck and powerful frame, Maximus's design was based on the Lipizzaner horse breed.

◀ This arcade game is the virtual home of Ralph, Felix, and other digital friends in concept art by Scott Watanabe.

Arcade Adventures

▶ Concept art by Wayne Unten shows Ralph in 8-bit video game style.

Video game stars new and old take to the movie screen in larger-than-8-bit style.

▼ Concept art by Helen Chen of Ralph sharing his mind with his fellow game-world residents.

What if a bully really wants to be a good guy for a change? Can he shake his rough-and-tumble reputation for a change of pace and gaming scene? That's what Ralph wants to know, and he's willing to risk his game station going "out of order" to find out. *Wreck-It Ralph* (2012) features a fun cast of classic arcade characters who pop in and out of the story of Ralph and his fellow fictional game characters Fix-It Felix Jr. and Vanellope von Schweetz. No matter what glitches and power outages may occur, Ralph and his companions come to each other's aid, learning to respect one another and themselves for their unique characteristics.

INTO THE INTERNET

The story of Ralph and friends continues in *Ralph Breaks the Internet* (2018). The characters' world broadens with access to the World Wide Web, making their trek from a broken gaming console in the arcade into an overwhelming universe of complex navigation options, complete with cloning and dark web complications.

◀ Game Central Station is a hub for all gaming worlds in *Wreck-It Ralph*.

◀ The world of Sugar Rush is not always as sweet as it looks, in concept art by Lorelay Bové.

▶ Cruising through the World Wide Web is an overwhelming mix of information and distraction, as Ralph and Vanellope encounter in *Ralph Breaks the Internet*.

High-Flying Fun

The "little plane that could" takes audiences to new heights.

"I can do more than what I was built for." DUSTY CROPHOPPER

◀ Dusty Crophopper has lofty goals in both of his big-screen stories.

Disneytoon Studios filled the big screen with two lofty stories about Dusty Crophopper, a small plane with big ideas and aspirations that soar way beyond the farming fields of his standard flight plan.

RISING UP

In *Planes* (2013), audiences are welcomed to Propwash Junction (which they may have momentarily visited in the 2011 *Air Mater* short) to meet Dusty in his home base, where he aspires to compete in the "Wings Around the Globe" competition. With the support of a dedicated crew, Dusty rises to the challenge, even overcoming his own fear of heights.

BLAZE OF GLORY

Champion Dusty faces his own mechanical shortcomings in *Planes: Fire & Rescue* (2014), and realizes a shift of career might be in order. He feels propelled to train as a firefighter to help support his hometown's needs, and he certainly feels the heat of that work when Augerin Canyon catches fire and his mettle is tested. Dusty comes through in a blaze of glory, proving once again that anything is possible, and blue skies are always within an optimist's sights.

▶ Dusty flies alongside Windlifter and Lil' Dipper to fight the blaze in *Planes: Fire & Rescue.*

Melting Hearts

Frozen enchanted audiences everywhere with an endearing snowman, two unconventional heroines, and one of the most spectacular gowns ever. One special song took the world by storm ...

◄ Development sketch of Olaf by Hyun-Min Lee

Inspired by *The Snow Queen* by Hans Christian Andersen, musical animated feature *Frozen* (2013) tells the snowy story of optimistic Anna and her epic journey to find her sister Elsa, whose icy powers have trapped the kingdom of Arendelle in an unending winter. *The Snow Queen* had tantalized Disney artists—including Walt Disney himself—several times over the decades. But it wasn't until 2008, when director Chris Buck suggested a musical version to executive producer John Lasseter, who had long been interested in the Andersen fairy tale, that the creatively iced up project started to thaw. Writer/Director Jennifer Lee—the first female director in Walt Disney Animation Studios feature film history—was inspired by the source material, particularly its theme of "love vs. fear" and she and the team created an original story from there. Once the filmmakers hit upon the idea that the heroine and the villain were sisters with a shared past, they realized the full potential of the story. Normal fairy-tale tropes were turned on their heads as the movie focused on the sisters' love for each other.

NORDIC ART DIRECTION

Art director Mike Giaimo drew on diverse Disney inspirations to create *Frozen*'s distinctive style. The design of Anna's traveling capes reflects patterns seen in costumes worn by Annette Funicello in *Babes in Toyland*, while the strong vertical and horizontal planes and bold use of color throughout the film evoke the stylized *Sleeping Beauty*. Giaimo traveled with his team to Norway to visit fortresses, castles, museums, cathedrals, fjords, and glaciers. The production design team found the natural environment, the architecture, and the traditional costume aesthetics perfectly suited to a Disney film they envisioned in the classic style.

SCORES OF ACCOLADES

Composer Christophe Beck skillfully infused Norwegian musical influences into the score, which was recorded by a full 80-piece orchestra featuring 32 vocalists, including Norwegian

Christine Hals, who provided authentic kulning, or herding calls. The songwriters—Kristen Anderson-Lopez and Robert Lopez—were deeply involved in the creation of the story. While building the plot, the filmmakers met with the duo every day. They

"We decided we didn't a traditional Disney

focused not just on the songs but also on the characters. The runaway hit "Let It Go" gives voice to Elsa's profound transformation. During the "Let It Go" number, Elsa transitions from buttoned up perfectionist

◄ Digital art exploring lighting, shapes, and character placement by assistant art director Lisa Keene.

▼ Elsa in her dazzling Snow Queen dress

to a person who gives herself permission to be who she is. Everything changes, including her hair, which becomes wilder, and her gown takes on a magical dimension. Elsa is finally free—even if she is alone.

want this to be princess song."
ROBERT LOPEZ

"Let It Go" won an Academy Award® for Best Song, while *Frozen* won the Oscar® for Best Animated Feature.

Into an Icy Unknown

▲ Concept art of the Earth Giants spirits by James Finch for *Frozen 2*

The warmhearted story of Elsa, Anna, and Olaf has sprinkled its frosty magic onto a heap of new adventures.

Frozen (2013) was the movie that took the world by storm. In *Frozen 2* (2019), the mystery of an Enchanted Forest is revealed, and the strength of both sisterly love and Elsa's powers is tested on a grander scale than ever before. The story takes place three years after the original film's timeline, with all the familiar characters present but slightly more mature in their look and behavior. Elsa and Anna are trying to figure out where they stand in the world as they embark on a quest to realize who they are meant to be in an emotional, action-packed, and melodic journey through Arendelle and beyond.

OPTIMAL OPTIMISM

Anna finds herself in a happy place at the start of the film, but as challenges arise, she realizes she has more to lose than ever before—and that she has to figure out how to do "The Next Right Thing" as the song conveys, one of seven new musical pieces created for *Frozen 2*.

THE POWERS THAT BE

No matter how happy Elsa is to finally embrace her powers and be with her sister Anna, their friends, and the people of Arendelle, she finds herself unsettled. A nagging voice in her mind cannot be ignored and it sets Elsa on a path of discovery beyond the safety of her realm. On this journey, she encounters the Water Nokk, a mythical water spirit that presents itself in the form of a horse who embodies the power of the ocean.

▲ Elsa rides the Water Nokk in powerful partnership.

"The music is fun but emotional, personal yet powerful, intimate but also epic." JENNIFER LEE (DIRECTOR)

▲ Concept art depicting the moment Elsa beckons to the unknown voice that is magically familiar to her in *Frozen 2*.

The character of the Water Nokk sprung forth from a combination of Nordic folk tales and the talents of Disney visual effects artists. *Frozen 2* also introduces characterizations of the spirits of earth, fire, and wind in its unique tale, plus a cast of new human characters that include Yelana, the strong leader of the Northuldra community.

PERMAFROSTED FUN

Since Elsa granted Olaf ever-frozenness with her magical powers, the endearing snowman has taken the spotlight in a number of fun shorts and series outside of his feature film roles. Created by the feature directing team of Chris Buck and Jennifer Lee,

Frozen Fever (2015) includes the original movie's voice talent and a brand-new song written by Kristen Anderson-Lopez and Robert Lopez. This warmhearted story packs a lot of fun into just seven minutes. Viewers can watch the people of Arendelle celebrate Anna's birthday, with party-planning mayhem from Kristoff, Sven, and Olaf, and many other magical snowmen. *Olaf's Frozen Adventure* (2017) is a musically

adorned tale, complete with four new songs and the important lesson of cherishing time-honored traditions in Arendelle. *Once Upon a Snowman* (2020) tells Olaf's origin story, and the spirited snowman also stars in a fun series of *Olaf Presents* (2021) interstitials, recounting Disney classics in his own special way.

▲ Baymax, the cutting-edge nurse robot, is transformed into a warrior with super-strength and the power of flight.

Brains, 'Bots, and Non-Stop Action

Dynamically combining anime-influenced design with cutting-edge computer animation, *Big Hero 6* is a Disney adventure unlike any before.

Based on a comic-book series, *Big Hero 6* (2014) centers on brilliant robotics prodigy Hiro Hamada, who finds himself in the grip of a sinister plot that threatens to destroy the city of San Fransokyo. With the help of a caring healthcare robot named Baymax, Hiro transforms a group of reluctant but supportive Applied Science students into a band of high-tech heroes.

BUILDING BAYMAX
The filmmakers decided early on that the heart of the film was the relationship between Hiro and the medical-care 'bot, invented by the boy's brother. Hiro's love of technology was inspired in part by Japanese researchers, who were all influenced by the robots seen in animation. In Japanese pop culture, robots are portrayed as the key to a hopeful future. Director Don Hall sought to present a robot never before seen on screen. Part of the process of creating compassionate Baymax involved researching the robotics world during field trips to MIT, Harvard, and Carnegie Mellon University in the U.S. and to Tokyo University in Japan. At Carnegie Mellon University, they witnessed research into soft robotics that included an inflatable vinyl arm. The minute the filmmakers saw the non-threatening arm, they knew they had their huggable robot. According to head of animation, Zach Parrish,

◄ The masked menace Yokai is a powerful and ruthless adversary.

many references were sought for Baymax's movements, including real and movie robots, cuddly babies, and koalas. With their long torsos and short legs—similar body proportions to Baymax—baby penguins were a particular source of inspirational moves and gaits. Fellow Director Chris Williams admits to loving "newborn" characters like Baymax who allow audiences to see the world anew through their eyes.

WAY OF THE WARRIOR
The "warrior" version of Baymax, upgraded by Hiro with a rocket fist, super-strength, and rocket thrusters, was given karate abilities by the *Big Hero 6* artists to broaden his skillset.

"It's really a hero's journey. The friendship Hiro forms with Baymax opens his eyes to what it really means to be a hero."

ROY CONLI (PRODUCER)

▲ The team's powers include super-speed maglev wheels, plasma blade weaponry, flight, balls filled with potent chemical agents, and steel-melting flames.

A few members of the team visited a nearby martial arts studio, where professional karate practitioners were asked to perform some of the movements while on their knees to simulate Baymax's signature proportions. In order to choreograph and execute the sequences of Baymax and Hiro soaring above the San Fransokyo skyline, filmmakers consulted with flight specialist Jason McKinley, who worked in the same role for Disney's *Planes*. As a result of the filmmakers' efforts, the movie won an Oscar® in 2015 for Best Animated Feature Film.

▶ An exotic mash-up of San Francisco's geography and Tokyo's energy, San Fransokyo makes an ideal location for this action-packed film.

▲ Many environments, architecture styles, and species coexist in Zootopia, as shown in this concept art by Matthias Lechner.

Life in the Urban Jungle

Animals of all shapes, sizes, and personalities go about their lives in a world never before seen by human audiences.

Young, ambitious rabbit Judy Hopps wanted to be a police officer all her life—and probably never imagined she'd team up with a scam artist fox, Nick Wilde, to solve her biggest breaking criminal case. The story of this unlikely duo plays out in *Zootopia* (2016), the 55th Disney animated feature that showcases animals in a mammal metropolis.

▼ Nick Wilde and Judy Hopps partner up on a clue-finding adventure.

"Even in an early pitch, Hopps and Nick had a great buddy dynamic. But I really wanted to tell this story because it's about bias and prejudice. It's important to discuss." JOSIE TRINIDAD (CO-HEAD OF STORY)

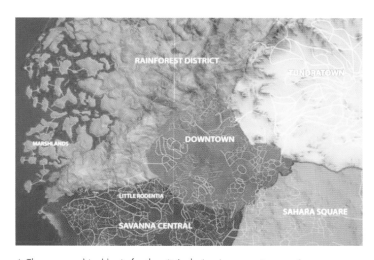

▲ The geographical logic for the city's design incorporates creative thinking in order to place dissimilar environments near each other, much like Disney's Animal Kingdom.

ANIMAL ARCHITECTURE

To create the city of Zootopia, Disney artists studied both wild animal populations and the development of cities, wanting the society of their Zootopian animals to be a natural blend of the team's findings. Of particular interest was the relationship between predator and prey, and also how deeply human tools, such as words, can become harmful tools. *Zootopia* was honored with an Academy Award® for Best Animated Feature among other accolades, and audiences can enjoy more animal tales from Zootopia in the streaming series *Zootopia+*.

▼ Animal hide and fur patterns are built into some of the cityscape in Zootopia, as shown in this concept art by Cory Loftis.

Waves of Wayfinding

Filmmakers dove into the history of the people and cultures of the Pacific Islands as deeply as the magnificent sea runs.

▶ Moana prepares with her parents for a meeting with the island's people.

I n her quest of self-discovery, young princess Moana is drawn to the ocean, and her personal expedition sets off a wave of inspiration to her whole community to regain their own proud voyager past. *Moana* (2016) is both the name of the main character and also the word for "ocean" in several languages from the Pacific Islands. A sixteen-year-old who exhibits courage, intelligence, and a desire that runs deeper than the ocean to find her true calling, Moana is a remarkably inspiring young princess who is willing to cast aside her royalty and others' expectations in order to find her authenticity.

▲ Toddler Moana and friendly wave concept art by Ryan Lang

WAVES OF EMOTION

The ocean itself is portrayed as a character in the film: director John Musker was strongly impacted by the Pacific Islanders' belief that "the ocean connects us. The land and the sea are one and the same." The design, technology, animation, and effects teams all worked together to craft the "shape language" (the look) of the ocean so that it would believably interact with Moana, and also generate a swell of emotional connection to the audience.

LIVING LEGEND

The magic of Disney computer-generated art was a vital element in how the moving tattoos and shape-shifting ability of demigod Maui played into the cinematic experience. Maui is a perfect character for the medium of animation, and one who is portrayed as larger than (human) life, and sometimes as an entirely different flying, crawling, or swimming creature. His tattoos reveal moments of his past and were a creative opportunity for the Disney animation and technology teams as his tattoos took on a life of their own—especially Mini Maui, a tattoo that acts as his conscience and was made with hand-drawn animation.

◀ Concept art of Maui by Jin Kim

SPIRITS ARISE

The blend of modern technology with cultural stories from the Pacific Islands added a depth of visual and sensory richness to the storytelling in *Moana*. The spirits of the ocean, volcano, and land are all expressed in character form, and the fantastical world that Moana discovers when she is afloat with Maui brings a whole other level of mythical storytelling to her journey.

"This connection to the past...is so important. It's encapsulated by a phrase we heard often, 'know your mountain.'" RON CLEMENTS (DIRECTOR)

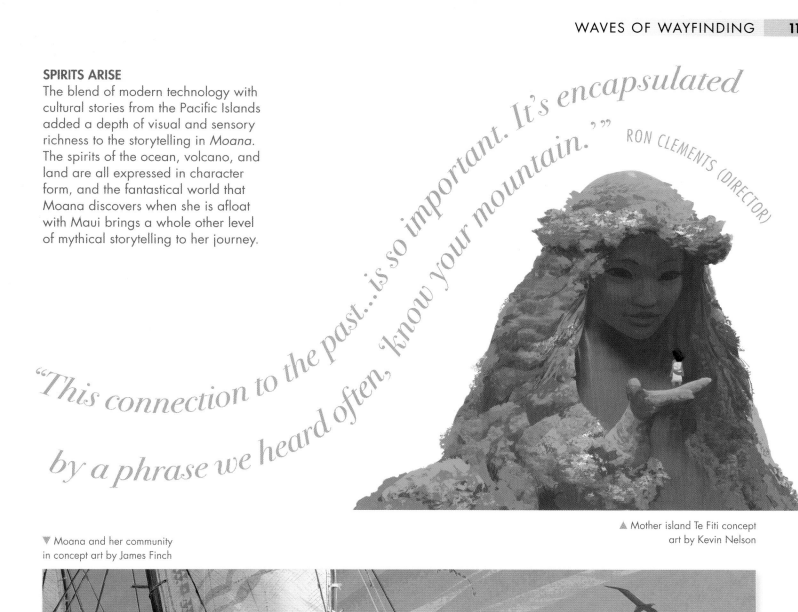

▲ Mother island Te Fiti concept art by Kevin Nelson

▼ Moana and her community in concept art by James Finch

Dragons and Druun

The bravery of a warrior princess set in a land inspired by the beauty of Southeast Asia makes for a fantastical adventure.

▲ Sisu and Raya work to become a mutually trusting pair.

▶ Raya rides Tuk Tuk, in a pill bug-inspired concept by Ami Thompson.

Raya and the Last Dragon (2021) is set in the fictional land of Kumandra, inspired by several Southeast Asian locations and cultures. Raya, whose name means "celebration" in Malay, is imbued with the passion and the personality needed to face a daunting task. When her land is overtaken by evil spirits, Raya must strike out on her own to find the long-hidden last dragon to help restore her community. Upon finding that dragon, Sisu, Raya gains a magical partner in her quest.

"...it's so rare that we get a major Hollywood movie with a special female friendship at the heart of it."   ADELE LIM (SCREENWRITER)

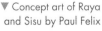

▼ Concept art of Raya and Sisu by Paul Felix

▲ The wondrous glow of Casita radiates magic and life. The house itself is an important character within the story.

The Magic of House and Home

When the joy of a family in an enchanted place is endangered, the most unexpected hero might shine.

The 60th Disney animated film shares the story of the Madrigals, who live in an amazingly magical house hidden in the mountains of Colombia. *Encanto* (2021) is a feast for the eyes, heart, and ears, coming to audial life with the music and lyrical work of Lin-Manuel Miranda. Inspired by magical realism, as real-world encantos (a term sometimes used for places in nature that are enchanted) are known to exhibit, the film takes audiences on a journey to explore the importance of family, and all of the unique individuals that come together to create such a powerful, magical force.

◀ Concept art of Mirabel in a beautifully and symbolically embroidered skirt reflecting each member of her family by Neysa Bové.

▲ Branches elegantly curve and intertwine in the Madrigal family tree by artist Lorelay Bové.

Exploring the Inner Frontier

The Avalonians have never known what lies beyond their community, until they find themselves in a strange world.

▲ The Pando plant, shown here in concep art by director Don Hall, is the wonder fue for the Avalonian community, generating an incredible amount of electrical energy

▲ Travel in Avalonia is all air-based, and the *Venture,* shown here in concept art by Paul Felix, is a prime example of its floating inflatable vehicles. In the Windy Jungle, imaginative vegetation is based on the shape of bronchial tree systems and mangroves.

When the energy source on which Avalonia depends is at risk, an expedition beyond the outer limits of their city brings the Clade family and President Callisto Mal into a very *Strange World* (2022). They discover environment after environment beyond their wildest imaginations, including the Windy Jungle, the Burning Sea, Luna Glade, and the Amber Desert, which are unlike anything they (and theatrical audiences) have ever seen. The landscapes and life-forms in this 61st animated feature from Walt Disney

Animation Studios are inspired in both look and function by key particles of living creatures, setting up a thoughtful story about interconnected survival on several levels.

GENERATIONAL GAP
The expedition also involves a deep dive into the relationships between family members, and specifically fathers and sons. The three generations of Clade men—father Jaeger, son Searcher, and grandson Ethan—each have different mindsets

and expectations for one another. Meaningful conversations among the trio about how behaviors, attitudes, and perspectives affect the present and the future are intermixed with love, humor, and incredibly imaginative, adventurous challenges, reminiscent of action-packed "pulp adventure" comics.

▼ Splat is an expressive and entertaining character despite the fact that it has no eyes or mouth, as shown in this concept art by Dan Lipson.

> "It's an imagined world that is a perfect allegory for our planet."
>
> ROY CONLI, PRODUCER

TO EXPLORE OR NOT TO EXPLORE

While Jaegar yearns for adventure, Searcher contrasts his father with his desire to stay literally grounded in farming. Ethan embodies both the excitement of exploring and an appreciation for the stability of his home, along with the company of his family, his crush Diazo, and his friends. Together each Clade evolves over time, much like the broader storyline about the environmental practices of their society.

BIO-INSPIRED

Like many biologically-inspired elements in *Strange World*, Splat is a creature based on an important part of the immune system, a dendritic cell. The design team looked at everything from gummy bears and soap bubbles to microscopic cells before they cooked up the final model. While its concept seems appropriately strange, Splat's appealing nature makes it huggable, which is fortunate since its few obvious bodily features include arms and legs.

▲ Ethan, Splat, Searcher, canine companion Legend, and Jaeger hang on for the ride—both physically and emotionally.

Wishing Upon a Star ...

The centennial year of Walt Disney Animation Studios in 2023 was also the year its 62nd animated feature, *Wish*, was released. Set in the magical kingdom of Rosas, the story introduces Asha, an optimist with a sharp wit who deeply cares about her community. When Asha turns to the sky in a moment of need and makes a wish, her plea is answered by a cosmic force—a little ball of boundless energy called Star. Together, with a pajama-wearing goat named Valentino, they face the most formidable of foes to save her community and prove that when the will of one courageous human connects with the magic of the stars, wondrous things can happen. It's like a wish come true for big-screen animation audiences!

A HOME FOR ANIMATION
Completed in November 1994 to accommodate production growth, the Feature Animation Building—now known as the Roy E. Disney Animation Building—was meticulously designed to meet every animation requirement.

WHERE LEGENDS MEET
Located outside Team Disney – The Michael D. Eisner Building, Legends Plaza hosts bronze plaques of many Disney legends who have significantly contributed to the legacy of The Walt Disney Company.

TWO OF A KIND
Sculpted by legendary Imagineer Blaine Gibson, the "Partners" statue of Walt and his old pal Mickey Mouse stands at the east end of Legends Plaza.

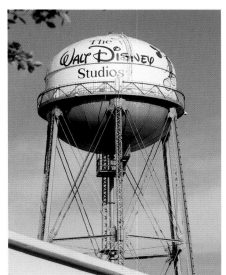

TOWERING TALL
The historic water tower soars 135 ft (41 m) high. Roy O. Disney considered the unique six-legged structure to be more aesthetically appealing than the standard four-legged towers.

Early exploratory sketches helped story artists get a feel for the film's characters and setting.

An animator's model of Albert Einstein, who has an encounter with the genius infant in the "Baby Weems" sequence of *The Reluctant Dragon* (1941).

Adjustable lamps could be moved in virtually any direction.

Models, such as this one of Sir Giles, were created to give the animators an idea of how characters should look.

THIS PICTURE IS MADE IN ANSWER TO THE MANY REQUESTS TO SHOW THE BACKSTAGE LIFE OF ANIMATED CARTOONS

The exposure sheet is a printed table that breaks down the film's action and serves as a timing guide for the animator.

A thin metal plate, or peg bar, holds the animator's paper in place to stop it from sliding.

The animation paper sits on a rotating disk that can be spun in either direction.

ANIMATION IN ACTION
A recreation of an animator's office from the early 1940s is on display at The Walt Disney Studios in Burbank, California. While the desk setup seen here highlights *The Reluctant Dragon* (1941), Disney archivists regularly update their displays to highlight new historical materials, and different eras.

The desk houses many of the animator's necessities with ample storage for their unique supplies.

Early Animator's Desk

To create the ideal artistic workstation, Walt worked with industrial designer Kem Weber to make special desks and furniture for the Disney animators. Housed in the Animation Building that served as the cornerstone of the Burbank studio, the animators' desks were where the Disney characters came to life. The impressive Art Moderne design of the desks provided an aesthetically pleasing environment for the artists, and the placement of the drafting area and drawers offered the ultimate in functionality. The first floor of the Animation Building was home to several of Walt's top animators—known as the Nine Old Men—who utilized these desks to create some of the most iconic animated films of all time.

ALL THE ESSENTIALS
Original animator's tools, including pushpins, erasers, and a Blackwing pencil were specially employed by Walt to assist the animator.

LET'S EAT
A Disney studio commissary menu from March 21, 1940 provides staff with the day's lunch options. Walt's Chili was often on the menu and remains so today.

Other Tools of the Trade

Walt Disney did not invent animation, as some people believe—he innovated it. In taking hand-drawn animation from a mere program-filler to an art form, Walt and his staff developed existing techniques and invented others, such as the storyboard. In order to better manufacture his unique product, Walt merged artistry with something of an assembly-line mentality—a step-by-step approach perfect for the animation studio that was affectionately known as "the Mouse factory." Here are just a few of the key tools and steps from the earlier days of the art form.

1A. STORYBOARDS
Conferences, such as this one seen in 1934, were held to present storyboards and review the story. This process allowed the directors and story artists to refine the action of the short or feature.

1B. PITCHING IDEAS
At a *Pinocchio* conference, Walt acts out the story using a series of storyboards to plan out the sequence. The Disney artists were always impressed with Walt's performances, saying he was as comedic as Chaplin.

2. LIVE MODELS
After the storyboards were approved, live-action reference footage was sometimes shot to assist the animators. Here, Kathryn Beaumont performs for *Alice in Wonderland*.

3. ANIMATION DRAWINGS
Supervising animators define the characters, from their final design to their onscreen performances. Here, Eric Larson "draws" inspiration from some spotted canine models. Creating the illusion of movement that gives life to a character, animators focused on key poses in a movement or action. Afterwards, a team of "In-betweeners" completed the necessary number of drawings for the 24 frames per second of on-screen running time.

4. INKED CELS
With nimble fingers and steady hands, the inkers traced the animation drawings— in ink, using the thinnest nibs available— onto clear celluloid sheets known as "cels."

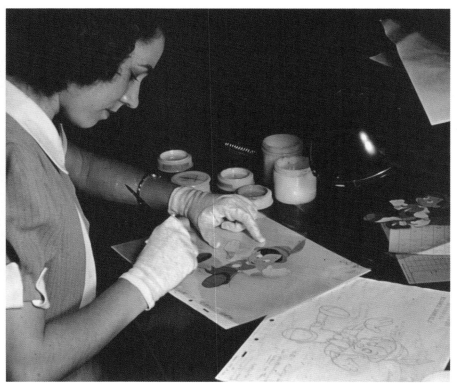

5. CUSTOM COLORS
At the Disney Paint Lab, custom-made colors were ground with a stone mill and mixed into hundreds of hues. These specially developed pigments made paints that photographed with true colors.

6. PAINTED CELS
Skilled painters swiftly applied the colors to the back of each inked cel. Each cel was then placed on a background under the animation camera to create one frame of film.

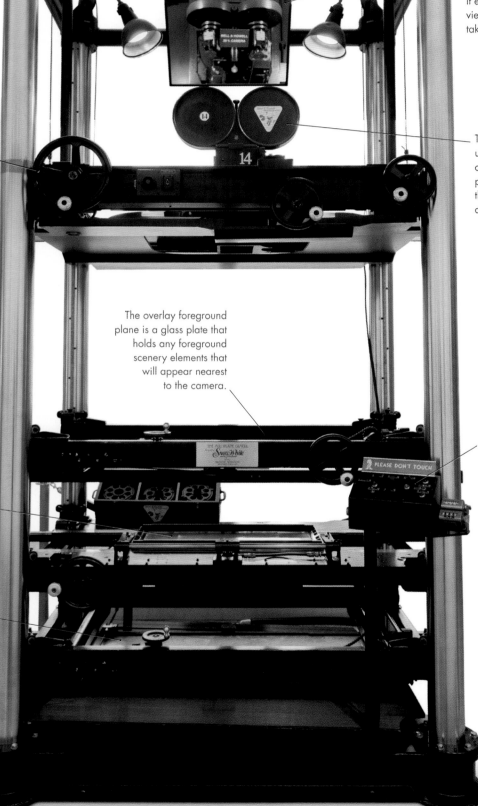

MULTIPLANE CAMERA
Disney's magical multiplane camera has a place of honor in the lobby of the Frank G. Wells Building, right next to the Walt Disney Archives. Though no longer used for production, this iconic artifact was one of the most important tools of the art of animation.

A mirror tops this elaborate animation camera crane to assist the technicians. It enabled the operator to view the film magazine take-up wheels.

The camera motor drive raises or lowers the camera carriage. The wheels can be used for manual adjustments.

The camera, moved up and down by the camera carriage, points down through the multiple levels of animation backgrounds.

The overlay foreground plane is a glass plate that holds any foreground scenery elements that will appear nearest to the camera.

The control box operates the camera shutter, the movements of the various planes, and the lights that illuminate the art so it may be photographed.

This contact plane or animation level is where character animation would be placed.

The lower background plane holds the final painting that serves as a backdrop for all the other planes.

The Marvelous Multiplane

Fantastical Disney environments such as *Bambi*'s idyllic forest or *Pinocchio*'s quaint village took on a new level of reality thanks to the wizardry of the multiplane camera. Under the guidance of Disney technical expert Bill Garity, a department of 18 skilled engineers invented this 14-ft (4.3-m) high crane that allowed background, middle distance, and foreground objects (painted in oil on large planes of glass or, for the bottom level, masonite) to be placed at different levels under the camera lens. It was developed for *Snow White and the Seven Dwarfs* but wasn't ready in time to be used exclusively. The multiplane camera was first used in the Academy Award®-winning Silly Symphony, *The Old Mill* (1937). The "marvelous multiplane" earned its creators a special Academy Award® in the Scientific and Technical category.

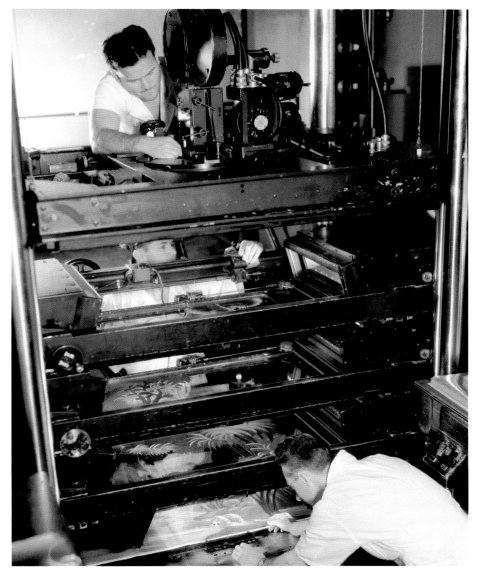

LOADING THE LAYERS
Disney Studio camera operators at work with the multiplane camera crane, 1940s. The multiplane camera required five to six technicians to operate. Each of the multiplane scenes took from two to three weeks to plan, involving many different elements from perspective to lighting.

THE FINISHED SCENE
From the completed film: Note the birds landing on the branch. The birds and the slender tree on the left are not part of the painting below as they were painted on separate pieces of glass as foreground planes.

BAMBI ARTWORK ON GLASS
The control, restraint, and subtle artistry of this masterful painting are all the more remarkable considering it is painted on glass.

In keeping with the atmospheric art direction of *Bambi*—inspired by Tyrus Wong's impressionistic pastels—details are suggested rather than rendered in detail.

More than just an indication of sky, patches of light are used in background paintings to direct the viewer's eye to the animated action.

A True Treasure

The multiplane camera was an important tool in expanding Walt Disney's cinematic storytelling vocabulary. Very few of the fragile multiplane backgrounds survive, so this one, showing the majestic forest in *Bambi* (1942), is one of the most precious treasures in Disney's Animation Research Library. There are multiplane shots throughout *Bambi*, but perhaps one of the most effective is a lengthy pan during the "Let's Sing A Gay Little Spring Song" number. It follows two blue jays as they fly through a springtime clearing to land on a blossoming branch.

While being photographed, the various multiplane levels move one-hundredth of an inch at a time. This pan stopped on this tree branch, the destination of the in-flight birds.

The backs of the glass planes were painted black to prevent light from the lower levels of the setup showing through the upper painting and spoiling the illusion.

Modern Tools

Walt Disney was all about innovation and improvement, and his legacy has carried on into today's animation processes at the studio.

Walt Disney Animation Studios has used its collective imagination not only in storytelling efforts, but also in advancing the art of animation through award-winning processes and technological breakthroughs. Teams of talented technologists support feature production through unique applications of an arithmetic expression language called SeExp (short for "Shared Expression"). SeExp translates into diverse digital tools to achieve artistic tasks, bringing a variety of animation styles to cinematic reality.

▶ **EVOLVING ANIMATION SOFTWARE**
In the 1980s, Disney technology teams and other experts developed the Computer Animation Production System (CAPS) which helped organize and track the progress of artwork through the animation pipeline, an innovation in the art process that earned an Academy Award® in 1992. Specific computer-generated animation elements had been worked into 2D animated films as early as the cauldron in 1985's *The Black Cauldron*. The celebratory rainbow sequence in 1989's *The Little Mermaid*

was a broader expansion of CG work via CAPS, refining processes and pushing boundaries to encompass all levels of animation in that section of the film. Disney produced its first fully CG film in 2005 with *Chicken Little*, and the animation group has continued to innovate and improve its digital workflow, as highlighted by a few of the more modern software examples shown here.

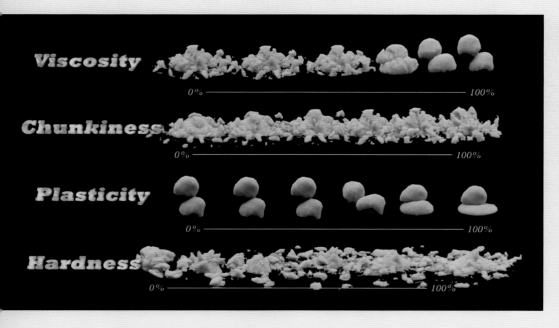

◀ **MATTERHORN**
This simulation tool is like an artists' version of being a physics professor: it can help model the behavior of blizzards, ocean waves, rainstorms, and mud flows and sand movement, among other complex visual effects. Olaf must be grateful for software like this—otherwise how would Elsa and Anna have had snow with which to build him? With computers helping to craft the ever-complicated algorithmic images that make up animated environmental effects, Disney artists can instead focus on molding those effects to fit the style of each film in which they are used, to tell each unique story with a unique look.

▼ MEANDER

This drawing tool helps artists merge computer-generated and hand-drawn animation techniques. It was first utilized in the Oscar®-winning short film *Paperman* (2012), and then again in *Feast* (2014), to create the linework accents. Meander was also utilized as the means through which KnowsMore's eyes were animated in 2018's *Ralph Breaks the Internet*, and, as shown here, to bring Te Kā, Maui's tattoos, and the tapa to animated life in *Moana* (2016). The tool has proven handy during work review sessions so that an animation supervisor or director can visually convey the shapes and motion they want to see in the final scenes on the big screen by drawing directly on the animation frames they are reviewing. The tech team that built Meander certainly have the gratitude of the artists that use it, but were also officially honored by winning an Academy of Motion Pictures Arts and Sciences' SciTech Award in 2017.

▼ FUR GROOMING

In the world of animation, the colors and textures of fur can be infinite. Mochi looks like the cat's meow in *Big Hero 6* (2014) thanks to the Disney developers who crafted a toolset to enrobe the Japanese Bobtail in all of his furry glory. Tools such as iGroom and Disney's XGen combine to create a robust, yet nimble toolset that artists use to sculpt grooms on characters, which can be easily modified for different types of fur. Such toolsets came in especially handy for *Zootopia* (2016) when the koala seen here and countless other animals portrayed an entire community of diversely furred characters.

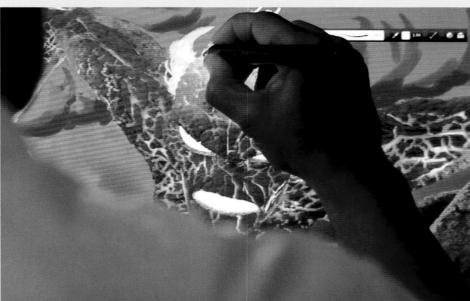

The Art of Sound

As seen with Mickey Mouse's debut in *Steamboat Willie* (1928), Walt understood the importance of sound at a time when many in the industry considered "talkies" a passing novelty. There had been sound cartoons before *Steamboat Willie*, but they commonly just played a phonograph record as the cartoon ran. Walt created a way to put a soundtrack on the film itself, allowing for the synchronization of action and audio. The blending of voices, sound effects, and music with the visual realized Walt's vision for an all-encompassing entertainment experience. Disney productions continue to innovate in the realm of soundscapes, but these fun peeks back in time provide a look at the trailblazing work of the studio.

VOICE ARTIST
Walt credited Cliff Edwards and his uniquely ebullient voice for helping make Jiminy Cricket a lovable presence in *Pinocchio* (1940) and more than 30 episodes of the *Mickey Mouse Club* television show.

QUACKTACULAR CLAMOR
Walt's creation of Donald Duck was inspired by voice actor Clarence "Ducky" Nash. Ducky provided the voice of the feisty fowl for more than 50 years.

MIGHTY VOICE
Pat Carroll puts her all into the booming voice of Ursula in *The Little Mermaid* (1989).

FROM VOICE TO TRUMPET
During production of *The Jungle Book* (1967), singer-songwriter Louis Prima performs with Sam Butera and The Witnesses.

THE SONGS SPEAK
The orchestra (right) assembles at the Disney studio to record music for *Bambi* (1942). The film has fewer than 1,000 words of dialogue, allowing the action and music to speak volumes. A large choir (below) sings the lyrical songs and acclaimed choral effects.

A NEW SOUND
Re-mixing for *Fantasia* (1940) took place at the new Disney Studios in Burbank, California implementing a stereo system called Fantasound developed by Disney in partnership with RCA.

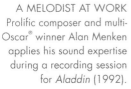

A MELODIST AT WORK
Prolific composer and multi-Oscar® winner Alan Menken applies his sound expertise during a recording session for *Aladdin* (1992).

▲ Bill Justice and Xavier "X" Atencio created vegetable characters for the Academy Award®-nominated *A Symposium on Popular Songs* (1962).

Spectacular Stop-Motion

Often a painstaking and time-consuming process, the stop-motion technique has been used to produce some of the most iconic Disney films to be seen on the big screen.

Walt Disney's first animated films in the 1920s were made with articulated paper figures brought to life through stop-motion animation. This painstaking process requires the animators to move each character incrementally, shoot one frame of film, and then move the characters again. In the late 1950s, animation director Bill Justice was experimenting with stop-motion, achieving a never-before-seen fluidity. As a result, Walt produced a fully stop-motion animated featurette, *Noah's Ark* (1959). The 150 characters in this Academy Award®-nominated film were constructed by Justice and fellow Disney artist Xavier "X" Atencio

from everyday objects such as corks, erasers, and golf tees. Walt asked Justice and Atencio to utilize the stop-motion technique for other films such as *Babes in Toyland* (1961). The toy soldiers in the "March of the Wooden Soldiers" sequence were about 12 in (30 cm) high with bodies cast out of hollow fiberglass, and each one was made with interchangeable sets of arms and legs. There were 40 soldiers in some scenes and each had 12 sets of legs. At every new frame, the legs on each soldier had to be placed at different angles to make one complete step.

STOP-MOTION SKELETON

Director Tim Burton has always had a fascination with stop-motion animation. While involved in the time-consuming process of creating the Disney short, *Vincent* (1982), he also planned a holiday stop-motion spectacular about a skeletal Pumpkin King who becomes obsessed with Christmas. *Tim Burton's The Nightmare Before Christmas* (1993) was originally a poem with concept sketches that set the visual

◀ Bill Justice works on the stop-motion sequence of *Babes in Toyland* (1961). The iconic toy soldiers returned in the "A Spoonful of Sugar" number in *Mary Poppins* (1964).

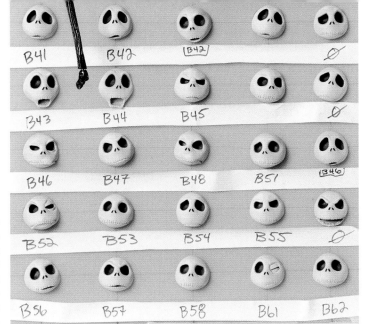

▶ Counting the duplicates that were made for backup, Jack Skellington from *Tim Burton's The Nightmare Before Christmas* (1993) had almost 800 different heads.

▼ A *Frankenweenie* (2012) sculptor works on the puppet of Mr. Rzykruski, who was designed as a homage to legendary horror actor Vincent Price.

and thematic tone for a feature film. Director Henry Selick used a 40,000 sq ft (430,560 sq m) vacant warehouse to accommodate the 230 sets and more than 227 animated characters. Most of the puppets stood about 1 ft (30 cm) tall, with a metal armature inside a foam body. All of the figures had multiple heads—the ragdoll Sally puppet had 120—with slightly different expressions or mouth positions. The film turned out to be the most extensive stop-motion production ever made.

HORROR ANIMATION
The story of a boy who uses Frankenstein-like methods to bring his dog back to life, *Frankenweenie* (2012) was originally directed by Burton as a live-action short back in 1984. But the filmmaker had always envisioned it as a full-length, stop-motion animated film. Burton modeled the characters in the style of classic horror films from the 1930s, and it took over a year to make with 33 animators using more than 200 puppets to create some of the most complicated puppets and scenes ever to be seen in a stop-motion animation.

"By using the magic of stop-motion photography we find that it's possible to give life to anything." WALT DISNEY

▶ Tim Burton "directs" the puppet of young Victor Frankenstein on one of the miniature sets of *Frankenweenie* (2012).

LUXO JR. (1986)
Pixar Animation Studios' first short, about two desk
lamps and a ball, was the first computer-animated
film to be nominated for an Academy Award®
in the category Short Film (Animated).

Early Days of Pixar

A collaboration between Walt Disney
Feature Animation and Pixar Animation
Studios took big-screen entertainment
to exciting new levels.

S ince the mid-1980s, Pixar Animation
Studios has evolved from a high-end
computer hardware company to a
powerhouse of imaginative and creative
filmmaking with an unbroken string of full-length
animated hits. Recognized for its collaborative
corporate culture—ideas are welcome from
anyone in the company—Pixar has successfully
turned everything from toys, monsters, and cars
into memorable characters. Each character has
human emotions that have moved and inspired
audiences worldwide.

PIXAR'S RENDER FARM
"Renderfarm" is Pixar's playful name
for the room that holds the 20,000
computers required to calculate
the colors, textures, and lighting of
each frame of the movies.

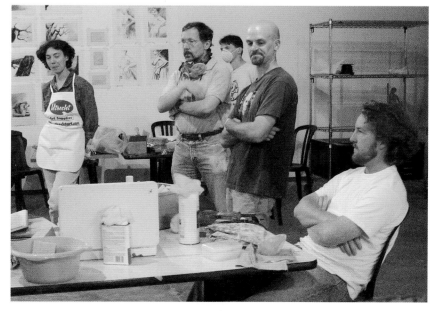

PIXAR UNIVERSITY
Pixar University, Pixar's internal
professional development program,
gives employees opportunities to
explore creative options beyond
their usual roles. Here, Ed Catmull
takes a sculpture class.

▲ Concept character sketches, like this one of Woody and Buzz Lightyear by Bud Luckey, are the starting point for a character's on-screen appearance.

▲ The late Pixar artist Bud Luckey with his concept sketch of Woody from *Toy Story*

▲ Supervising technical director William Reeves working on Woody.

▲ Andy's heart is full of love for his favorite toys, Buzz and Woody, in *Toy Story*.

▼ Woody is reunited with the Roundup gang in *Toy Story 2*.

▲ *Toy Story 3* passes the love of favorite toys onto a new generation, as Andy bestows his beloved collection on to Bonnie.

▼ Woody and Buzz share a moment at the carnival as Woody prepares to rustle himself a new path and purpose in *Toy Story 4*.

TECHNO-TAINMENT

In the mid to late 1980s, the filmmakers at Pixar Animation Studios experimented with award-winning short films and assembled their teams and technology in preparation for their first feature-length computer-animated film. Simultaneously, the leaders at Walt Disney Feature Animation were looking for ways to diversify their productions beyond traditional two-dimensional, hand-drawn animation. When the two studios collaborated, the result was a movie that is now considered a major milestone in animated filmmaking— *Toy Story* (1995). Four years in the making, the warm and humorous tale of two toys vying for a young boy's affection was the first full-length computer-animated feature film. Giving audiences a toy's-eye view of the world, the film made Pixar a household name and inspired three hugely popular feature-length sequels: *Toy Story 2* (1999), *Toy Story 3* (2010), and *Toy Story 4* (2019); a spin-off movie *Lightyear* (2022); and a series of fun short films.

◄ Buzz Lightyear as seen in *Lightyear*, the origin story for the heroic space ranger who inspired the iconic toy.

Magical New Heights

Pixar Animation Studios brought new magic to animated storytelling with stunning visual style and emotional depth.

▲ The ants pile up their goods on the offering stone in *A Bug's Life*, as depicted in visual development by Tia Kratter and Nat McLaughlin.

True to the Pixar storytellers' penchant for choosing unusual subjects, their next film, *A Bug's Life* (1998), opened up the world of insects to viewers with a colony of ants, a troupe of down-on-their-luck circus bugs, and some very bad grasshoppers. In making the film, Pixar storytellers pushed the boundaries of computer technology to create natural, organic shapes and characters that squashed and stretched. Setting up new technical challenges seemed to become standard operational procedure at Pixar, as long as the technology served the story. Technological advances used for *Monsters, Inc.* (2001) included a breakthrough depiction of fur and hair to make Sulley, whose world is turned upside down by a human toddler— another believable monster. When Sulley and Mike went back in time to *Monsters University* (2013) the technology that made that prequel possible had advanced once again— for example, the 2013 version of Sulley had approximately 5.4 million hairs, which was about five times more than he had in *Monsters, Inc.*

HEARTFELT STORIES

Moving from a world inhabited by monsters to one populated by fish, Pixar storytellers once again took computer-animation technology to new heights to create the underwater world of *Finding Nemo* (2003) and refined it again for *Finding Dory* (2016). Whether they are using technology to animate human characters, like *The Incredibles* (2004) and *Incredibles 2* (2018), or machinery as in *Cars, Cars 2*, and *Cars 3* (2006, 2011, 2017),

◀ A vivid character concept sketch by Ricky Nierva emphasizes the shapes of Sulley, Mike, and Boo.

▼ A young and wide-eyed Mike Wazowski takes in the awesomeness of life at Monsters University.

▲ Dory and Nemo get along swimmingly in *Finding Nemo* and *Finding Dory*.

▲ Lighting pastels by Ralph Eggleston explore lighting—and by extension color, staging, and character for a sequence in *Finding Nemo*.

it is always a tool and never an end in itself. Like an animator's pencil of the past, computer animation serves one purpose—to create believable worlds and tell stories that come straight from the heart.

FAMILY DYNAMICS

The Incredibles movies follow the story of the Parr family, who deal with relatable real-world issues while contending with the call to use their superpowers. Recognizing their own self-worth and finding a work-life balance is hard enough to manage without having to also save the world from time to time, but the Parr family approach these challenges with a depth of humor and emotion that connects with people of all ages.

▼ *The Incredibles* was the first time Pixar animated an entire cast of human characters.

EMOTIVE MOTORING

Meaningful relationships shift through high-speed adventures for Lightning McQueen in the *Cars* trilogy. Whether he is redeeming his racing career, solving an international caper, or facing his own mortality, McQueen has to navigate many obstacles to find his way to happiness, self-fulfillment, and loyalty to his friends. Lightning does so in such an authentic way that audiences find themselves cheering as McQueen tears up the roads and racetracks.

▶ *Cars* co-director Joe Ranft found the perfect inspiration for Mater in a vacant lot in Galena, Texas.

▼ Mater and McQueen become best buds, even though they come from different sides of the road.

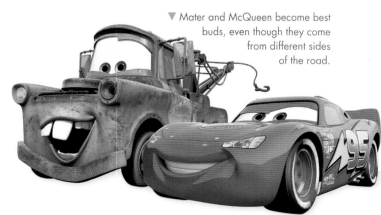

Characters with Heart

Whether robots, rats, or humans, there's a foundation of real emotional truth to all Pixar's characters.

▲ Remy can walk upright and use his forepaws for cooking, as seen in this colorscript study by Harley Jessup.

◀ Remy dreams of becoming a chef in *Ratatouille* (2007).

Since becoming part of The Walt Disney Company in 2006, Pixar storytellers have continued to create characters that resonate emotionally with moviegoers. The Pixar stories frequently explore one particular overarching theme: a character yearns for a goal, and with the help of friends or family, ventures into the world to seek it and learns to appreciate their loved ones along the way—a universal, timeless theme that touches the hearts of audiences.

LOVABLE CHARACTERS

In *Ratatouille* (2007), Remy, a young rat, has an impossible dream. He wants to become a chef—in a culinary world that obviously does not welcome rats in the kitchen. To make their rodent star appealing, animators studied real rats at length and layered their innate cleverness and natural sense of curiosity into Remy's character.

"*When you have characters with big obstacles to overcome, that's really juicy stuff for animators.*" BRAD BIRD (WRITER-DIRECTOR)

▼ Remy and Linguini partner to cook up critic-worthy cuisine.

▲ Story artist Brian Fee works on a *WALL•E* storyboard. Storyboards help filmmakers hone the characters' stories and emotional arcs.

EXPRESSIVE ROBOT

A sense of yearning pervades *WALL•E* (2008), the story of a rusty little trash compactor, who, left alone on Earth for years, meets a sleek seeker robot named EVE and follows her across the galaxy. Despite the fact that WALL•E's speech is limited, the animators were able to evoke different emotions using his eyes, whose design was inspired by binoculars. They kept his movements simple to convey his playfulness and wonder, which help audiences believe that a machine is capable of a deep and noble love.

▲ WALL•E's eyes evoke different feelings when tilted at different angles, as shown in this lighting study by John Lee.

◄ It's love at first light for WALL•E when he meets EVE.

REAL-LIFE EXPERIENCES

Pixar filmmakers often draw upon emotional experiences for their work. In *Up* (2009), they captured the emotions of Carl, who wants to have one last adventure, and Russell, the naïve young boy who accidentally accompanies him. While creating both characters, the filmmakers coined the term "simplexity"—a combination of simple design with complex emotions. Carl's facial expressions are considered the most subtle and sophisticated of all Pixar characters to date.

▼ Concept art from *Up*, such as this painting by Ricky Nierva, helps define both the look and personality of determined Carl Fredricksen.

▲ Shading Art Director Bryn Imagire and Director Pete Docter discuss rock formations during an *Up* art review.

Eons of Emotion

Whether returning to old friends or introducing new ones, Pixar storytellers have always searched for the characters' motivating emotions.

▲ Pencil sketch depicting Merida's dramatic red hair by Matt Nolte.

As wild as the landscape around her, Princess Merida of Castle DunBroch refuses to let anyone—especially her mother, Queen Elinor—decide her destiny. She is determined to hunt it down for herself. In *Brave* (2012), Merida is thoroughly bored by her mother's lessons on how to behave like a princess and would much rather be galloping her horse, Angus, over the Scottish Highlands, or practicing archery. Finding the delicate balance in Merida's personality—between her teenage rebellion and her yearning for her mother to listen to and understand her—was a challenge. But as mother and daughter struggle to break Queen Elinor's enchantment, they weave a deeper bond that frees Merida to at last find her own destiny.

WILD LOCKS

The animators of *Brave* wanted to give Merida a look that communicated her exuberance and energy—enter her wild, fiery red hair. Merida's hair has its own way of reacting to her emotions, and it moves with such life that it is practically a character itself.

◄ Steve Pilcher's dramatic image of Merida and Elinor as a bear was the first painting created for the movie.

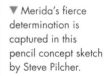

▼ Merida's fierce determination is captured in this pencil concept sketch by Steve Pilcher.

SON-SHINE

Following a twist of evolutionary history, in which dinosaurs still exist in the modern world, *The Good Dinosaur* (2015) shares an emotional story in an *Apatosaurus*-sized way. Arlo has a hard time "making his mark" in his world, and finding his own value. His dramatic journey of self-discovery challenges him to display courage he never knew he had, and ultimately leads Arlo back to the family that values him more than he ever realized.

▲ Realistic landscapes, based on the geography of the Northwestern U.S., invite audiences to feel welcome in an otherwise unfamiliar story setting of prehistoric creatures in modern times in *The Good Dinosaur*.

▶ Arlo and his young companion Spot find unexpected friendship and a renewed sense of family together.

▲ Characters Anger and Disgust look at Riley's memory shelf in *Inside Out*.

FEELINGS IN FRAME

In *Inside Out* (2015), Pixar depicts human emotions as actual characters, giving them shape, color, and personalities. Joy, Sadness, Anger, Disgust, and Fear personify and enact what audiences had only ever felt and not seen on a movie screen before. Their animated presence in the mind of a young girl named Riley conveys the story of what moving to a new place sometimes feels like ... from the inside out.

▼ Pixar artists had a unique challenge in personifying human emotions for *Inside Out*. After all, no one knew what they looked like—until now.

Around the Globe, and Beyond

From Mexico and New Mushroomton to the Great Before, Pixar shares inspiration and joyful storytelling from all corners of the universe.

▲ Concept art of Miguel by Zaruhi Galstyan

Full of the vibrant color and energy of Mexico, *Coco* (2017) is a story of reconciliation and the importance of honoring both the legacy of the past and the beauty of the present. Miguel loves his family, but also secretly has a love of music that plays into a fantastic reunion with his ancestors on Día de Los Muertos. The Pixar team even figured out how to make non-fleshed, skeletal characters emotive, as seen in the Land of the Dead realm, and their work was honored with an Academy Award® for "Best Animated Feature," while "Remember Me" by Kristen Anderson-Lopez and Robert Lopez won the Oscar® for "Best Original Song."

> *"We always knew we wanted to end the film with a moment that married music with memory; it felt like the only way that we could make Miguel's journey complete."* JASON KATZ (STORY SUPERVISOR)

▲ Miguel and Hector strum up a multigenerational musical jam.

▶ Miguel at a cross-existence family reunion in concept art by Zaruhi Galstyan

▲ Ian and Barley concept art by Matt Nolte

▲ Conjuring Dad did not go exactly as hoped.

ROAD TRIPPIN'

Elfin brothers set out on a journey full of spells and magic in *Onward* (2020), but at the heart of Ian and Barley's story, their true transformation comes when they find closure with their deceased father Wilden, and know they have earned his pride.

Artistically, the Pixar team dazzled audiences by conjuring an entire world of fantasy, carefully crafting what magic looks like in the *Onward* world.

THE SOUNDTRACK OF LIFE

Set in both New York City and the Great Before, *Soul* (2020) follows the story of Joe Gardner, set in the rich backdrop of the world of jazz. On a deeper level, Joe's journey challenges his perspective on what living a meaningful, enjoyable life could be, and even inspires another soul named 22 to embrace and embody her will to live. The film was honored with an Academy Award® for "Best Animated Feature" and another Oscar® for "Best Original Score."

◄ Middle-school music teacher Joe Gardner ponders a jazzier career.

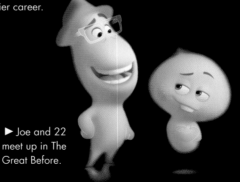

► Joe and 22 meet up in The Great Before.

▼ The Counselors share their otherworldly perspective with Joe and 22 in The You Seminar.

"Almost any moment in our lives could be a transcendental moment that defines why we're here." PETER DOCTER (DIRECTOR OF SOUL)

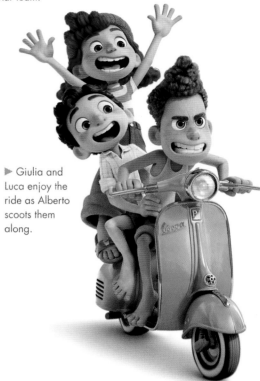

The town of Portorosso is a blend of the Cinque Terre area of Italy with a childlike sense of summertime vibrancy and magic, as constructed by the Pixar team.

▶ Giulia and Luca enjoy the ride as Alberto scoots them along.

Friendship, Fur, and Fire

Whether on land, in the sea, or somewhere in between, Pixar shares inspiration and joyful storytelling from all corners of the universe.

The Italian Riviera is known for its fantastic beauty, but in *Luca* (2021) it can also become a fantastic place where sea creatures and humans interact. Luca and Alberto know what it's like to feel different, or excluded, but they learn how much richer life can be when you step out of your comfort zone to explore other cultures, while honoring and sharing your own. Together with Giulia, Luca and Alberto realize that the power of friendship is bigger than preconceived notions of people they don't know.

"It's a love letter to the summers of our youth—those formative years when you're finding yourself." ENRICO CASAROSA (DIRECTOR)

▶ Luca and Alberto form an unlikely friendship, becoming the best of friends through their adventures together.

▲ Panda Mei, Abby, Miriam, and Priya channel their teen energy into singing along to their favorite band's song "Nobody Like You."

PANDA PROBLEM

It's hard enough to channel emotions for any teen, but it's extra work when losing control of one's emotions could turn a girl into a red panda. This is the cursed life that Meilin "Mei" Lee faces in *Turning Red* (2022), but she eventually learns to appreciate that the curse may actually be a blessing, and how she is meant to live her most authentic life. *Turning Red* is a humorous and heartfelt tour through teendom's ups and downs, including all the emotional spikes along the way.

"We're all imperfect, and this character needed to reflect that."

RONA LIU (PRODUCTION DESIGNER) ON PANDA MEI

◀ Meilin learns to appreciate her unique traits in both versions of herself.

▶ Fern Grouchwood processes tickets in his office in *Elemental*.

EVERYTHING IN BALANCE

Opposites react in Disney and Pixar's *Elemental* (2023) where water, fire, land, and air residents live together in Element City. Fiery Ember befriends go-with-the-flow Wade and together they embark on an adventure that unexpectedly challenges long-held beliefs.

▶ Wade and Ember enjoy a stroll in Element City.

Pixar Easter Eggs

Playful Pixar artists embed visual in-jokes in their films as a treat for themselves and their most attentive audiences. Known as "Easter Eggs," these references are cleverly concealed, or sometimes "hidden in plain sight." They include cameo character appearances, visuals of props, titles of previous works, or places and events from Pixar history. A few of the Easter Eggs, such as the Pizza Planet truck and "A113" are Pixar perennials, and the artists who hide them have hatched an entire cadre of eagle-eyed fans who pride themselves on finding every one.

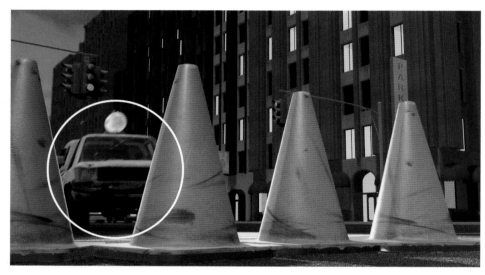

TOY STORY 2 (1999)
The yellow Pizza Planet truck that first drove onto the silver screen in *Toy Story* (1995) appears again in *Toy Story 2* when the toys drive it to the airport.

UP (2009)
In homage to Pixar's much-loved first feature, the Pizza Planet truck appears in every subsequent Pixar and Disney•Pixar movie. In *Up*, it makes a cameo appearance in the fantastic sky-high view of the street from Carl Fredricksen's soaring residence.

BRAVE (2012)
How do you add a truck to a film that is set in medieval times? Possibly the crafty Witch has seen into the future—and made a carving depicting a vehicle from it.

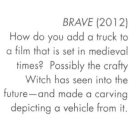

FINDING NEMO (2003)
In an homage to the animation classroom at Cal Arts, where the director of *Finding Nemo*, Andrew Stanton, and other notable Pixar directors attended, the number A113 appears in every feature. Sometimes audiences have to dive deep to spot it, such as in *Finding Nemo* where it appears as the model number on a diver's camera.

A BUG'S LIFE (1998)
In the bugs' world vision of Broadway, New York, a quick glimpse of *The Lion King* show's logo is visible.

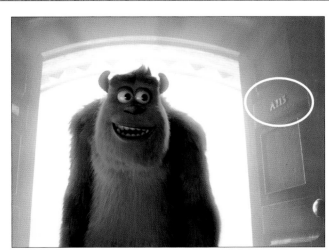

CARS (2006)
The cinematic big race shuts down the town of Emeryville, which also happens to be the real-world location of Pixar Animation Studios.

LUCA (2021)
A plush toy of a Disney icon sits quietly leaning against the bedpost in Giulia's room—perfect for an Italian setting since Donald Duck has been a widely popular character in Italy for decades.

MONSTERS UNIVERSITY (2013)
The use of A113 comes full circle from its reference to the CalArts classroom where Pixar animators studied hard, to Sulley's first college classroom—where he does not.

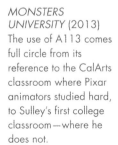

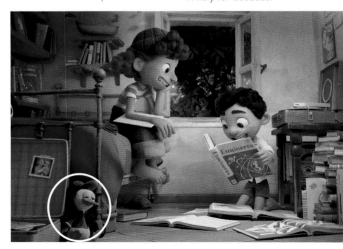

Short and Sweet

Walt Disney's short films date all the way back to the very beginnings of his animation career and continue to be a tradition for innovative storytelling over a century later.

The body of work known as the Alice Comedies were some of the earliest shorts Walt created at his studio, which encompassed 56 such examples. The charming *Steamboat Willie* (1928), the first fully synchronized sound short, and featuring the debut of Mickey Mouse, was an historically notable cinematic achievement, and the Silly Symphonies soon followed,

encompassing 75 shorts, seven of which won Academy Awards® for best cartoon. Mickey Mouse, Donald Duck, Goofy, and Pluto have since appeared in some combination or solo-starred in hundreds of shorts from the 1930s to 1950s, with hundreds of other fun characters following in their cartoon path. There are now over 500 animated shorts in the Disney film archives,

and more than 100 beyond this when the Pixar collection is counted. The practice of creating shorts allows new filmmakers to test their mettle, and innovative technologies and processes to be explored, all for the betterment of the art form. Here is a selection of the diverse animated shorts crafted through the years, proving that good things do come in small packages.

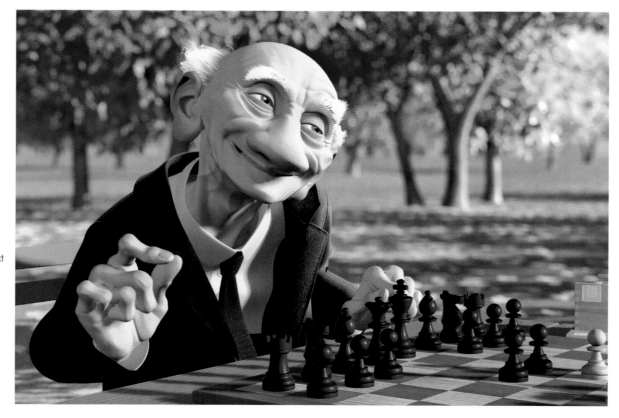

► *Geri's Game* (1997) was the first Pixar project to have an elderly human as a main character, and Geri was loosely based on director Jan Pinkava's own chess-playing grandfather. The short won an Academy Award® for "Best Short Film (Animated)."

◀ A story of love and destiny is portrayed in Walt Disney Animation Studios' *Paperman* (2012), which also received an Academy Award® for "Best Short Film (Animated)."

▲ *Feast* (2014) provides a dog's-eye view of human love, and served up an Academy Award® to Walt Disney Animation Studios for "Best Short Film (Animated)."

▲ Motherly love for a son is the main course of the deliciously heartwarming story of *Bao* (2018) from Pixar, which was also honored with an Academy Award® for "Best Short Film (Animated)."

▶ Like all Pixar shorts, *Burrow* (2020) was pushing the boundaries, this time with its charming 2D look. It follows the struggles of a young rabbit who is trying to build her perfect home.

TV Toons

Disney animation provided even more fun, adapted for the small screen and broadcast right into the audience's living room, or streamed on their personal viewing device in more recent times.

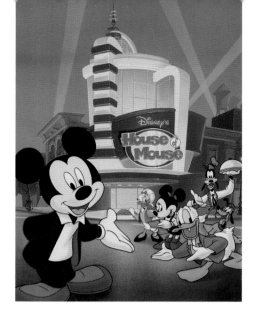

▲ Mickey Mouse and his pals welcomed TV audiences, as well as a host of Disney animated stars, to the fun at *House of Mouse*.

With the rise of cable television and the increase of TV channels in the 1980s, Michael Eisner and Frank Wells were determined to bring quality Disney animation to television on a regularly scheduled basis. Eisner had once overseen ABC's Saturday morning animation programming and wanted at least one new series on TV by the end of 1985—and right on schedule, *The Wuzzles* and *Disney's Adventures of the Gummi Bears* appeared as part of the 1985–1986 schedule. Not long after, *The New Adventures of Winnie the Pooh* premiered in 1988 and became the first of any Disney series to win the Emmy® Award for Best Animated Program, Daytime, in both 1989 and 1990.

QUALITY ANIMATION

These shows were produced on a bigger budget than other animated TV shows at the time so they could live up to the Disney name. One product of this first wave of creativity was *DuckTales* (1987), featuring the syndicated escapades of ultra-wealthy Scrooge McDuck and the gang from Duckburg. This five-days-a-week series was so successful, as was its spin-off, *Darkwing Duck*, that Disney created *The Disney Afternoon* in 1990, with *DuckTales* as the linchpin of a two-hour animation block. Other popular shows were *Chip 'n' Dale Rescue Rangers* (1989), *TaleSpin* (1990), and *Gargoyles* (1994). Mickey Mouse himself made a return to the small screen in two Saturday morning animated series, *Mickey MouseWorks* (1999) and the variety show *House of Mouse* (2001). Over the decades, Disney audiences have experienced a wide variety of worlds and adventures through animated series, and here are just a few more examples of the fun scenes on screens of all sizes.

◀ *DuckTales* brought the exploits of Scrooge McDuck and much of the Duck clan from the Carl Barks comic-book series to animation.

▶ The preschool series *Sofia the First* (2013) is the tale of a young princess in training, and explores what makes a real princess—the inner qualities of kindness, generosity, loyalty, honesty, and grace.

▶ *Handy Manny* (2006) and his singing tools shared vibrant lessons on collaboration and being helpful in one's community.

◀ *Doc McStuffins* (2012) introduced more complex storytelling and characters to preschool television, with Doc helping kids to understand what's happening at the doctor's office as she treats broken toys in her neighborhood.

▶ *Elena of Avalor* (2016) was an inspiration to young audiences—portraying life lessons about compassion and leadership—and also earned several Daytime Emmy® Awards.

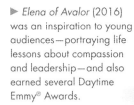

▼ Penny Proud and her family have come to entertain and educate multiple generations of fans, with *The Proud Family* debuting in 2001 and *The Proud Family: Louder and Prouder* launching in 2022.

▲ *Phineas and Ferb* (2007) follows the fun of two young brothers as they embark on ambitious and creative projects—fun that expanded into feature-length films and a live touring show.

"*I do not make films primarily for children.*
I make them for the child in all of us,
whether we be six or sixty." WALT DISNEY

Disney in Action

▲Alice (Margie Gay), Walt Disney, and a few
of their friends from the animated world who
show up in the Alice Comedies.

Bridging Between Worlds

Part of the magic of Walt Disney was his ability to tell fascinating stories successfully in different formats—be they animation or live-action, long-form or short-form, or some combination thereof.

When the imagination of Disney artists combines the animation and live-action methods of entertainment into a hybrid form, that magic is intensified into a deeper audience experience, making them wonder if they, too, might encounter a flying dragon or a talking mouse when they walk out their front door. From the earliest Disney hybrids, the crossover of animation and live-action proved to be a remarkable innovation in both filmmaking and entertainment, perpetuated through the decades to come.

SILENT BUT SILLY

Walt's hybrid production, the pilot film *Alice's Wonderland*, was his first to combine live-action and animated characters within a cinematic reality, and the 56 cartoons that followed in the Alice Comedies series continued the blended adventures of live-action Alice and her animated counterparts, like Julius the cat, and the dastardly Pete.

INSECT INTERSTITIAL

One of the "package features" that Walt Disney created in the 1940s, *Fun and Fancy Free* (1947) combines live-action segments with the presentation of two cartoons, "Bongo" and "Mickey and the Beanstalk." The hybrid hijinks are provided by animated Jiminy Cricket as he explores a live-action home, making himself comfortable while setting up a record player. Large-scale crossover fun comes at the end of the film, when Willie the Giant emerges from his fairy tale and heads off to real-life Hollywood.

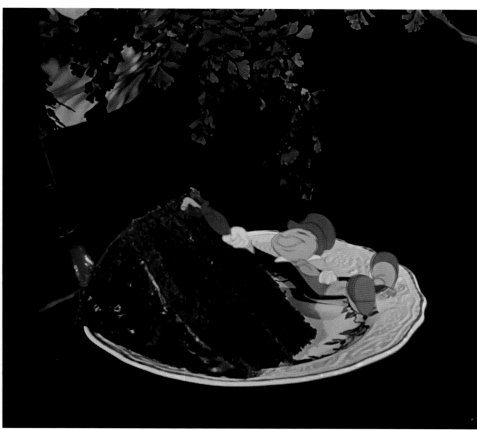

▲ ◄ Animated Jiminy Cricket enjoys music and dessert at young actor Luana Patten's birthday party, and Willie peeks into the scene as well in *Fun and Fancy Free.*

Practically Perfect

Walt Disney combined unforgettable performances, lilting songs, and wondrous movie effects into one of Hollywood's biggest hits, *Mary Poppins*.

With astounding special effects overflowing from a bottomless carpetbag of movie magic, *Mary Poppins* (1964) is an extravagant musical fantasy about the proper British nanny who can do anything. She can slide up a banister and sing a duet with her own mirror reflection or pop into a chalk pavement picture for tea and cakes. Walt knew this unique fantasy was an ideal subject for Disney special effects to bring to life in a movie musical. He first became intrigued by this extraordinary character in the early 1940s when he found his daughter Diane laughing as she read the first of the *Mary Poppins* books by P. L. Travers. He finally obtained the screen rights in the early 1960s, and assigned songwriting siblings Richard and Robert Sherman to weave the stories into song. One of the first and most significant songs, "Feed the Birds" was inspired by a story Mary Poppins tells the children in her care about the elderly Bird Woman who sells bread crumbs at St. Paul's Cathedral. The Sherman Brothers saw the story as deeply spiritual; a gentle plea for charity and love.

▲ The magical nanny floats over the rooftops of London, the world of the chimney sweeps.

"We decided to try something that would employ about every trick we had learned in the making of films ... in an enormous fantasy— Mary Poppins. " WALT DISNEY

CASTING A NANNY AND A CHIMNEY SWEEP

In 1961, Walt saw Julie Andrews in her Broadway hit, *Camelot.* He visited the star backstage and launched into an all-out rendition of the *Mary Poppins* story. Later, Julie agreed to make her motion-picture debut as the enigmatic nanny. It was Walt's idea to combine several different characters from the original books into Bert, a jack-of-all-trades who is a one-man band and a chimney sweep, among other occupations. The great showman ultimately cast Dick Van Dyke, the versatile star of the stage and film musical *Bye Bye Birdie* and the classic television series, *The Dick Van Dyke Show,* in the role of the happy-go-lucky friend of Mary Poppins.

WALT'S GREATEST ACHIEVEMENT

By combining all the eye-popping movie magic at his command—from live-action, animation, and music to comedy, sentiment, and *Audio-Animatronics®* technology—Walt brought *Mary Poppins* to cinematic life. When it debuted on August 27, 1964, the movie was a huge hit. It was nominated for 13 Academy

▲ The toy blocks from the children's nursery are now housed in the Walt Disney Archives.

▲ Mary Poppins (Emily Blunt) is responsible for her young wards Georgie (Joel Dawson), Annabel (Pixie Davies), and John (Nathanael Saleh) in *Mary Poppins Returns.*

Awards® and won five Oscars®, including Best Actress for Julie Andrews. A true classic, it's no wonder that *Mary Poppins* was known as "Walt Disney's Greatest Film Achievement."

This achievement inspired future cinematic celebrations, including the live-action *Saving Mr. Banks* (2013), as well as another hybrid film, *Mary Poppins Returns* (2018).

A Spoonful of Storyboard

A Disney-developed practice for visualizing the action of a film, the first complete storyboards were drawn up for the Silly Symphony animated short *Three Little Pigs* (1933). Walt Disney credited artist Webb Smith for inventing the concept of drawing scenes on separate sheets of paper and pinning them up on a bulletin board to develop a story in sequence. But storyboards are not just for animation; Disney has long utilized the technique for live-action movies. Storyboards were created for the entire *Mary Poppins* film including the "A Spoonful of Sugar" sequence. Stop-motion specialists Bill Justice and Xavier "X" Atencio planned the eye-popping special effects through the storyboard process, too.

ORIGINAL STORYBOARD
Credited with "Nursery Sequence Design" in the film's opening titles, veteran Disney artists Bill Justice and Xavier "X" Atencio storyboarded *Mary Poppins'* magic as she tidied up the nursery to the tune of "A Spoonful of Sugar."

AUDIO-ANIMATRONICS® BIRDS
The robins who whistle the merry song along with Julie Andrews were created by *Audio-Animatronics®*, Disney's own technology of three-dimensional figural animation. This innovative process was then in its early stages and was creating a sensation at the 1964–1965 New York World's Fair the same year *Mary Poppins* was released.

A Creative Encore

Bedknobs and Broomsticks reunited the creators of *Mary Poppins* to conjure up show-stopping musical numbers, live-action and animated antics, and the magical misadventures of an amateur witch.

▲ "The Isle of Naboombu" prop storybook is preserved in the Walt Disney Archives.

Angela Lansbury stars in this musical extravaganza as prim and proper Miss Eglantine Price, who just happens to be taking a correspondence course in witchcraft. Miss Price reluctantly teams up with three young Cockney orphans and a conman—played by Disney favorite David Tomlinson—to find an ancient spell to help save England from invasion in World War II. Amazingly, the origins of this Oscar®-winning film actually predate *Mary Poppins*, as Walt Disney obtained screen rights to *The Magic Bed-knob* and *Bonfires and Broomsticks* by English author Mary Norton in the 1940s. However, it was not until the 1960s, during a dormant

period in the development of *Mary Poppins*, that Walt, songwriters Richard and Robert Sherman, writer/producer Bill Walsh, and co-writer Don DaGradi began crafting a screen musical. These moviemaking magicians took the basic idea of a sorceress and combined it with an idea from a 1940 newspaper story that Walsh remembered, which speculated about British witches staving off Nazi invasion. "The Old Home Guard" was the first tune the songwriting Shermans composed for *Bedknobs and Broomsticks* (1971) because they felt strongly that the film was really about the spirit of England. Most of the *Bedknobs* songs and

▲ Filming the Oscar®-winning special effects using the Disney-perfected sodium vapor process, or "yellowscreen," which is similar to the famous bluescreen process.

story material were created in conjunction with Walt during this early period. When work resumed on *Mary Poppins*, Walt temporarily set *Bedknobs* aside.

BRINGING IT ALL TOGETHER

Flash forward to 1969, three years after Walt's death, when Bill Walsh revived the project. Setting out to fulfill Walt's original vision, he reunited the *Mary Poppins* team, including director Robert Stevenson, and cast Angela

◀ Publicity art showcasing the hybrid of cartoon critters and real-life action.

Lansbury, fresh from her Broadway triumph in *Mame*. The film was shot at the Disney Studio on lavish sets including a three-block recreation of London's famed Portobello Road. The animated soccer match was directed by one of Walt's legendary Nine Old Men, Ward Kimball, and features 130 gags at a breakneck pace. *Bedknobs and Broomsticks* premiered in London on October 7, 1971, at the famed Odeon Theatre in Leicester Square.

The sorcery-filled super-spectacular was nominated for five Academy Awards® (including Best Song for "The Age of Not Believing"), and its eye-popping onscreen magic won the Oscar® for Best Special Effects.

"There's kind of a nice, homey, folksy quality about an English witch" — BILL WALSH (PRODUCER/CO-WRITER)

▼ Miss Price's magic bedknob (aided by Disney's Oscar®-winning special effects) takes the spell-seekers to the bottom of an animated ocean.

Worlds Collide and Coexist

A magical blend of animation and live-action can bring fun of all sizes into theatrical reality, be it on dragon or chipmunk scale.

▲ *Pete's Dragon* is a magical, musically-brightened story of friendship and loyalty told in a big screen, big character way.

The beloved Elliott made his screen debut in *Pete's Dragon* (1977) as the invisible friend and guardian of a young orphan, Pete. Often creating more complications than solving them—but always acting with a pure heart—Pete eventually makes himself visible so that those who follow the "I'll believe it if I see it"motto can accept his presence. In 2016, a new version of *Pete's Dragon* graced theater screens, set in the Pacific Northwest instead of New England, and featuring more trees and fewer songs than its predecessor.

▼ Elliot (who has a new look and new spelling in 2016) and 10-year-old Pete together in the wild

HAPPILY EVER AGAIN

Enchanted (2007) blends classic-style animation and modern live-action to create a wholly unique adventure. Would-be princess Giselle (played by Amy Adams) is tricked by the evil Queen Narissa and banished from her fairy-tale kingdom to modern-day New York City. An animation veteran, director Kevin Lima knew that this Disney homage was the perfect project for him. The filmmakers had always planned *Enchanted* as a musical in the Disney tradition, and Amy Adams and James Marsden (who plays Prince Edward) were aided in Disney-style vocalizations by voice coach John Deaver. The dancing in the ballroom scene was choreographed by John

"Cha-Cha" O'Connell, who referenced waltzes performed in the ballroom sequences of Disney animated movies such as *Cinderella* (1950) and *Beauty and the Beast* (1991). The story of what happens when the fairy tale merges with the real world ten years later is further explored in *Disenchanted* (2022), as Giselle tries to live a suburban life in Monroeville, but is drawn back to Andalasia to face even greater challenges than that of raising her teenage stepdaughter.

▲ In the animated segment of *Enchanted* (2007), Queen Narissa disguises herself and throws Giselle into a well and into reality.

▲ As seen in their 1989 versions, Chip and Dale may not look like they serve in an underground international investigative agency, but that just means they are doing their jobs as Rescue Rangers well!

> *"We tried to let the script speak back to all the traditional Disney movies."*

KEVIN LIMA (DIRECTOR, ENCHANTED)

TWO OF A KIND

Continuing from where the hit animated series left off, the 2022 film *Chip 'n Dale: Rescue Rangers* brings a fresh look to the big screen. It is the ultimate hybrid film in mixing both 2D and 3D characters into a live-action world. Acknowledging their co-starring roles in a show 30 years prior, but having fallen out and grown apart since, Chip and Dale—the former appearing as a traditionally animated character and the latter now in computer-generated style—must reunite for a daring rescue.

▶ In *Disenchanted*, Giselle turns into a wicked stepmother after her wish for her family to have a fairy-tale life goes disastrously wrong.

▲ The dynamic duo may have new looks, but they still embody the same fun partner-in-solving-crime vibe in the 21st century.

▲ Bobby Driscoll in London during his 1950 *Treasure Island* publicity tour

A Live-Action Treasure

The adventure movie that launched a thousand movies, *Treasure Island* got Walt's all-live-action career off to a swashbuckling start.

Though he had originally considered *Treasure Island* (1950) as an animated feature in the late 1930s, Walt Disney soon changed his mind, planning the pirate property as an animation and live-action combination, with Long John Silver spinning animated animal yarns for young Jim Hawkins. But the Disney Studio had frozen funds in England: box office receipts earned by Disney films in the UK could not be exported due to postwar currency regulations. Walt decided to spend the funds in England, sailing into uncharted waters by producing *Treasure Island* as his first all-live-action feature film.

FILMING IN ENGLAND

Exteriors were shot at Denham Studio near London while the sea scenes were filmed at Falmouth in Cornwall. For the seagoing scenes, an 1887 three-master schooner was rebuilt and outfitted with two concealed diesel engines. Walt also enlisted master British matte painter Peter Ellenshaw. The artist added ship masts and other visual elements through paintings on glass panes placed in front of the camera during filming. Later, at Walt's invitation, Peter joined the Disney Studio in California, contributing to such classics as *Mary Poppins* (1964).

CLASSIC PERFORMANCES

Walt long had his young contract player Bobby Driscoll in mind to play Stevenson's stouthearted hero, Jim Hawkins, just as soon as Bobby reached the right age to play the cabin boy. The recipient of an Academy Award® for Outstanding Juvenile Performance in 1949, Bobby was the only American (and the only child) in a cast otherwise filled with British performers, chief among them the brilliant stage and film actor Robert Newton. Having already won acclaim working with such esteemed filmmakers as Alfred Hitchcock, Laurence Olivier, and David Lean, Newton turned in an indelible performance and a career-defining role as the rascally Long John Silver.

◄ The tropical-looking beach was actually in a studio in London, England.

▼ Disney star Bobby Driscoll as heroic cabin boy Jim Hawkins and Robert Newton in his signature role as Long John Silver

▶ Map detailing the location of pirate Captain Flint's lost treasure.

"Buried treasure, pirates, excitement, and adventure— all these combine to make Robert Louis Stevenson's Treasure Island *one of the best known—and best loved—adventure stories of all time."* WALT DISNEY

JUST THE BEGINNING

After its world premiere in London on June 22, 1950, *Treasure Island* was released on July 19, 1950. The film was a hit—so much so that Disney set sail with three more swashbucklers filmed in England, including *The Story of Robin Hood and His Merrie Men* (1952). Though he would of course continue with his animated features and shorts, Walt Disney was now undisputedly a live-action filmmaker.

Oceans of Adventure

From two great fabulists—Walt Disney and Jules Verne—surged *20,000 Leagues Under the Sea*, one of Hollywood's most acclaimed science-fantasy epics.

▲ The crew films underwater with specially augmented cameras.

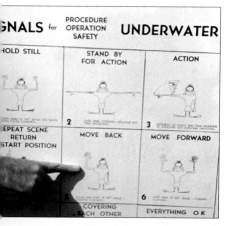

▲ Disney-designed hand signals chart for underwater filming

The inspiration for one of Walt's greatest live-action classics actually began with his award-winning True-Life Adventures nature documentaries. Visualizing an undersea True-Life Adventure storyboard, production artist Harper Goff created a sequence drawn from *Twenty Thousand Leagues Under the Sea* by Jules Verne. Fascinated, Walt decided to produce *20,000 Leagues Under the Sea* (1954) as his first made-in-Hollywood blockbuster live-action feature.

WALT'S INNOVATION
20,000 Leagues was only the second movie to be produced in CinemaScope® and a custom waterproof case for the cameras and the CinemaScope® viewfinder was devised. To encompass the mammoth production, Walt had constructed a huge new sound stage on his studio lot, Stage 3, which included a massive indoor tank.

THE STAR OF THE MOVIE
Walt cast the film from among Hollywood's best. Top box-office star Kirk Douglas was signed as bold harpoonist Ned Land, and James Mason delivered a powerful

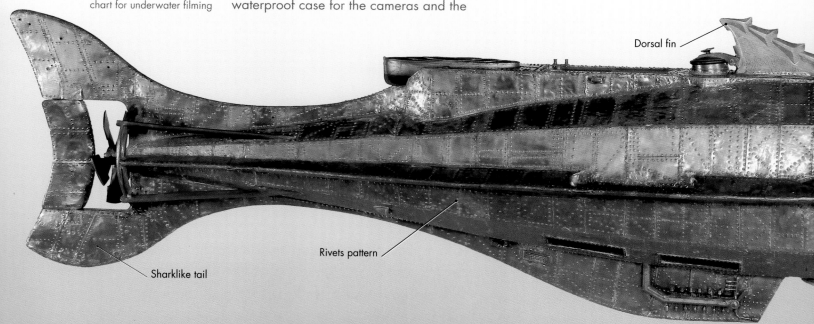

Dorsal fin

Rivets pattern

Sharklike tail

◄ James Mason as Captain Nemo in the amazing squid battle scene

as was a full-size *Nautilus*, which was 200 ft (61 m) long and 26 ft (8 m) wide at its broadest point. The mechanical two-ton (2,000 kg) squid that battled the mighty *Nautilus* had eight 40 ft (12 m) long tentacles and required a team of 28 to operate.

UNDERWATER MOVIEMAKING

Filming began January 11, 1954, with the underwater footage filmed on location in the crystal clear waters of Nassau in the Bahamas. For eight weeks, a 54-member crew shot more underwater footage than had ever been seen in a film up to that period, with the crew limited to 55 minutes at a time underwater due to the amount of oxygen in their air tanks. Disney's diving and design experts invented unique but practical costume diving suits: hand-tooled outfits weighing a staggering 225 lb (102 kg).

performance as tormented undersea genius Captain Nemo. To Harper Goff, however, the star of the film is Nemo's atomic-powered submarine, the *Nautilus*. The artist's starting point in envisioning this Victorian-styled vessel was its supposed appearance as a sea monster. Its streamlined body, dorsal fin, and prominent tail simulated features of a shark. The heavy rivet patterns on the surface plates represented the rough skin of an alligator, while the forward viewports and top searchlights represented its menacing eyes. Six scale models of the sub were used in the filming,

"When we decided to make a picture out of this classic story, we soon discovered that the imagining was much easier to do than the doing." WALT DISNEY

Viewports

▼ Captain Nemo's undersea ship, the iconic *Nautilus*

Anchor

Favorite Classics

Over the years, Walt and his namesake studio produced a myriad of live-action motion pictures, many of which are true Disney classics that have stood the test of time.

The kaleidoscope of classic live-action films created by Walt through the years is part of the enduring Disney legacy. The wide variety of subjects includes the leprechauns in the fantasy *Darby O'Gill and the Little People* (1959), which originated from the great showman's fascination with the Darby O'Gill stories by H. T. Kavanagh. In the 1940s, Walt visualized the film as a combination of animated leprechauns and live actors, but by the 1950s, he saw it as a spectacle of live-action effects.

▲ One of Disney Studio's biggest stars of the 1950s and 1960s, Tommy Kirk shone in *Old Yeller*, a coming-of-age story about a boy and his dog.

▼ A lavish song-and-dance spectacle in the grand Hollywood tradition, *Babes in Toyland* was Walt's first all live-action musical.

"... we have never lost our faith in family entertainment—stories that make people laugh, stories about warm and human things ..." WALT DISNEY

MAGICAL EFFECTS

Walt challenged his filmmaking wizards to make the tiny leprechauns completely believable, a task that called for painstaking planning. By placing Darby (played by Albert Sharpe) in the foreground and the actors playing leprechauns much farther back and lower, the camera perspective convincingly made it look as though the wily old storyteller was interacting with the Little People. The intense special effects used for *Darby O'Gill and the Little People* called for an extremely well-lit set, and so much electricity that one particularly complex shot caused a citywide power failure in Burbank.

ENDURING CLASSIC

Classic Mother Goose characters and an entrancing vision of a Toyland where wooden soldiers come to life have made *Babes in Toyland* (1961) a holiday perennial. Disney composer George Bruns enlivened Walt's vision by adapting the beloved melodies from Victor Herbert's original stage hit into an Academy Award®-nominated movie score. Annette Funicello is the film's leading lady. Disney's "girl next door" from TV's *Mickey Mouse Club*, she was then at the peak of her success as a recording star. For the comically villainous Barnaby, Walt cast Ray Bolger, the Scarecrow in MGM's *The Wizard of Oz* (1939).

CRUCIAL CASTING

Walt cultivated his own stable of stars that in addition to Annette, included Tommy Kirk, who turned in a deeply affecting performance in *Old Yeller* (1957) and Hayley Mills, who made her Disney debut in *Pollyanna* (1960), an adaptation of Eleanor H. Porter's novel. Kurt Russell may hold the longevity record, having appeared in Disney live-action and animated productions for over five decades, starting with *Follow Me, Boys!* (1966), through the Dexter Riley series of films including *The Computer Wore Tennis Shoes* (1969), and more. Long after her memorable performance in *Mary Poppins* (1964), Julie Andrews came back into the Disney fold as royalty in *The Princess Diaries* (2001) and its sequel in 2004.

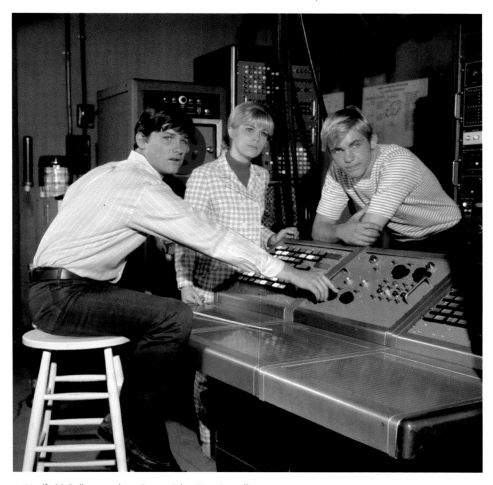

▲ Medfield College students Dexter Riley (Kurt Russell), Annie (Debbie Paine), and Pete (Frank Webb) gain more than just a technology donation in *The Computer Wore Tennis Shoes.*

Clever Comedies

Disney comedies earned a place
in cinema history with a distinctive
blend of slapstick, fantasy,
and innovative special effects.

Walt reveled in creating cartoon-like antics in live-action films. The result was a series of comedies combining slapstick, special effects, and a soupçon of social satire. Walt had originally planned *The Shaggy Dog* (1959) as a TV show, but when the network wasn't interested, he produced it as a theatrical feature instead. Starring Disney favorite Tommy Kirk as the teenager-turned-canine, this wacky live-action funfest also featured Fred MacMurray in his first Disney film. The sight of a big, furry dog driving a car, brushing his teeth, and performing other

◀ Fred MacMurray mastered the science of slapstick in *The Absent-Minded Professor.*

human activities was a crowd-pleaser and *The Shaggy Dog* became one of the biggest box-office hits of the year.

SHOWSTOPPING EFFECTS

MacMurray returned in *The Absent-Minded Professor* (1961), the story of Medfield College's Professor Ned Brainard, who discovers an anti-gravity material—flying rubber—that he dubs "Flubber." The airborne-automobile effects in the film utilized a number of filmmaking techniques, including the matte process (where actors and background footage are combined), miniatures, and wire-supported mock-ups. The basketball game scene, featuring the Medfield basketball team bouncing high over the heads of their rivals, took two months to shoot. As well as trick shots mixed together, the scene used an all-new approach to create the illusion of flight by suspending actors on wires. *The Absent-Minded Professor* was such a hit that Walt produced a popular sequel, *Son of Flubber* (1963), and decades later, his studio crafted an updated version starring Robin Williams in 1997.

SCIENTIFIC MISHAPS

Walt's comic traditions carried into decades beyond his time on the set, as seen in such films as *Honey, I Shrunk the Kids* (1989). This blockbuster

◀ *The Shaggy Dog* put a teen-turned-pooch in the driver's seat, fueling a whole series of special-effects comedies.

"A family picture is one the kids can take their parents to see and not be embarrassed." WALT DISNEY

depicts a big problem for inventor Wayne Szalinski when his children and the neighboring children are accidentally shrunk by his scientific creation to a minute size, and must face a series of misadventures to return home.

HO HO HUMOROUS

Scott Calvin (played by Tim Allen) is not looking for a new job when he dons the Santa suit, but inadvertently inherits a very famous one due to *The Santa Clause* (1994). Scott's accidental career detour brings lots of joy to children around the world, whether he likes it or not. The joy continues as Scott learns about the "Mrs. Clause" in *The Santa Clause 2* (2002) and considers what he needs to do as he nears retirement age in the streaming series *The Santa Clauses* (2023).

▲ MacMurray returned as Prof. Brainard in *Son of Flubber*.

Amok! Amok! Amok!

The three sisters Sanderson first flew onto cinema screens in *Hocus Pocus* (1993). Winifred (Bette Midler), Sarah (Sarah Jessica Parker), and Mary Sanderson (Kathy Najimy) are sibling Salem sorceresses who were resurrected by the lighting of the Black Flame Candle, and are ready to avenge their deaths and regain their youthful presence. In the wake of this magic theatrical moment, the film—full of Halloween hijinks and humor—became a classic Disney comedy with a seemingly bewitched following. Families and fans around the world have made watching *Hocus Pocus* a hallowed holiday tradition.

The sisters are brought back to the screen after their seemingly fiery demise in 1993 by another lighting of the mystic Black Flame Candle, this time unknowingly by a young teenager, Becca, in the Salem Woods … and thus the dead arise—as well as a whole new adventure for Becca and her friends. *Hocus Pocus 2* (2022) is a fun-filled story of sisterhood between teen friends and, in the case of the Sandersons, actual sisters. The film also sweeps two catchy tunes into its witchy storyline, "The Witches are Back" and a Sanderson-ified version of the 1970s classic song "One Way or Another."

The sequel was shot in the towns of Providence, Rhode Island, and Boston, Massachusetts, but production designer Nelson Coates cast his spell of theatrical trickery on those locations to make them into a Salem village as it would have appeared in 1653.

The Forbidden Woods were created within the Cranston Armory Stage and contained more than 90 hauntingly handcrafted trees made of fiberglass and silk leaves over a steel structure, planted among devilishly designed rock formations. Coates worked his magic again in Newport, Rhode Island to craft the Salem Scare Fest, which also involved costume designer Salvador Perez concocting 600 unique costumes to dress the townsfolk. Sarah, Winifred, and Mary Sanderson are hauntingly radiant in new costumes designed by Perez, while their original *Hocus Pocus* attire is housed in the Walt Disney Archives. Their sequel capes each use 26 yd (24 m) of double-layered silk Habotai fabric covered in tiny Swarovski Crystals.

▶ Eight black cats performed the role of Thackery Binx in the original film, trained by Larry Madrid. He also worked with Hickory, who played Cobweb in the sequel.

Illuminating the Digital Frontier

A futuristic sci-fi adventure set in a video-game universe, *Tron* is a revolutionary experiment in computer-generated images.

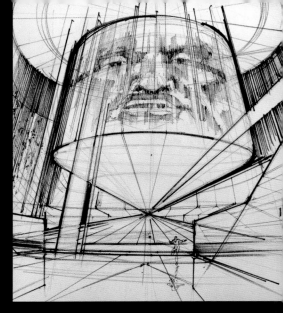

▲ A story drawing for the Master Control Program, one of the first characters in cinematic history realized through computer-generated imagery.

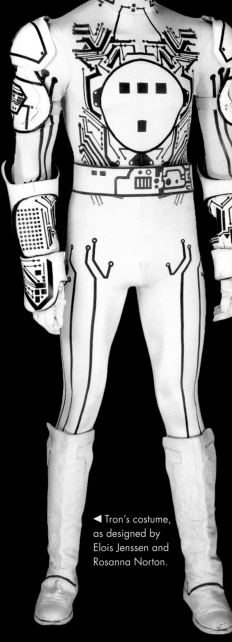

◄ Tron's costume, as designed by Elois Jenssen and Rosanna Norton.

Tron (1982) foresaw the digital revolution and gained a dedicated fan base fostered by the growing popularity of video games. In the film's sci-fi story, video game designer Kevin Flynn (played by Jeff Bridges) finds himself trapped inside a computer where he is forced to compete in life-or-death video games by the evil Master Control Program (MCP). In a daring plan, Flynn teams up with Tron, a rebel program, to challenge MCP for control of the computer world, his only hope of returning to the real world.

TALENTED TEAM

The genesis of this electronic epic began in 1975, when writer/director Steven Lisberger saw his first video game. Lisberger found himself intrigued by the uncanny, lifelike quality of computer graphics. Armed with his inspiration, Lisberger assembled a top-flight creative design team including comic book artist Jean "Moebius" Giraud, visual futurist Syd Mead, and special effects wizards Richard Taylor and Harrison Ellenshaw (matte painter and son of Disney special effects wizard Peter Ellenshaw). Together they developed the look of the futuristic vehicles, costumes, and scenery as they would appear in the digital world of *Tron*.

BACKLIT TECHNIQUE

During pre-production, Lisberger decided to use video compositing to create the illusion of real actors (who

"I realized that I could use computers to tell a story about video games. The games were the basis for the fantasy; the computer imagery was the means to create it."

STEPHEN LISBERGER (WRITER/DIRECTOR)

► To achieve the glowing effects on the characters, (1) the actors were photographed in black and white; (2) special matte cutouts were made of each frame; (3) painted backdrops and the circuit glow were added in post-production which create what the crew called "backlit animation."

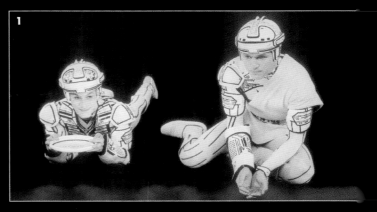

performed against plain black backgrounds) in a world made of electricity. By photographing in black and white, then reprocessing the film using colored filters and backlit animation (a process whereby colored light is shone through cutouts in animation cells), live characters took on a glowing design that effectively linked them with their surroundings in the electronic world.

SPECIAL EFFECTS SPECTACULAR

The intensive postproduction process of combining computer-generated imagery with the live-action footage took ten months to complete. *Tron* required 1,100 special effects shots with 200 of those incorporating live-action—the most ever used up until that time in a non-animated feature. 48 million bits of information were needed to complete a single frame, each frame requiring up to six hours to render.

THE SEQUEL

Seven years in the making, *Tron* was released on July 9, 1982, to critical acclaim for its groundbreaking visual effects. The enduring popularity of the film among its passionate fans inspired the sequel *Tron: Legacy* (2010). Like its predecessor, *Tron: Legacy* was a triumph of special effects, pushing the boundaries of new technology. The virtual reality of The Grid aimed for a more advanced version of cyberspace, and director Joseph Kosinski was determined to make the audience feel like filming actually occurred in the fictional universe. This meant building several physical sets and using a variety of special effects techniques. Cameras were also specifically designed to shoot The Grid sequences entirely in 3D.

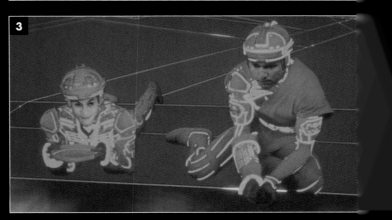

▼ The original Lightcycle scenes required both computer-generated graphics and traditional animation to create the illusion of programs racing inside a computer.

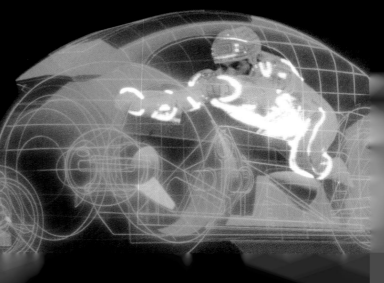

Rocketing into Adventure

A thrilling adventure in the air, *The Rocketeer* zoomed into the hearts of sci-fi and comic-book fans to become a high-flying cult classic.

Comic-book action, pulp magazine adventure, and movie serial suspense combine to create high-octane adventure in *The Rocketeer* (1991). Young test pilot Cliff Secord is hurled into a daring adventure of mystery and intrigue in 1938 Los Angeles when he discovers a top secret rocket pack that allows him to navigate the skies as the mysterious helmeted hero the Rocketeer. Reminiscent of 1930s TV adventure serials, the film is based on a comic-book series introduced in 1981 by writer-artist Dave Stevens (who has a cameo in the movie as a German test pilot).

DYNAMIC DESIGN

A fan of the original comic book, director Joe Johnston strove for lots of action in the movie, but also authenticity in recreating the look of the period. The design of the film required hundreds of technicians to recreate a 1938 Los Angeles. In addition to building period sets—including the

▶ Artist and sculptor Edward Eyth designed sets, props, storyboard sequences, and the iconic rocket jetpack.

The Rocketeer's jetpack emitted real fire trails from its thrusters.

A functioning engine was included in the prop jetpack.

A leg guard was added to the pack for the safety of the stunt performers.

The jetpack could be easily dismantled to make adjustments to the engine.

pup-shaped Bulldog Café, based on an actual Los Angeles restaurant— designing the all-important Rocketeer costume was a challenge. The designers reimagined the rocket pack from its original comic-book design, giving it a more aerodynamic, functional look. The Rocketeer's helmet had to appear practical as well as dynamic in design, and dozens of variations were drawn up. Finally, just a week before filming was due to begin, Stevens worked with sculptor Kent Melton to create the sleek, streamlined headgear that is seen in the movie.

STARRING ROLE

In casting for the role of Cliff Secord, hundreds of actors were considered (even Dave Stevens himself was invited to audition). But it was Billy Campbell, the physical embodiment of the youthful test pilot as seen in the comic, who was finally selected to play the Rocketeer.

"I was intrigued by the comic-book character, the period in which it is set, and what I knew would be a great adventure story."
JOE JOHNSTON (DIRECTOR)

HIGH-FLYING EFFECTS

The special effects wizardry in the film had to be effective enough to convince an audience that a rocket-powered man could fly, and required much preparation. To create the illusion of flight and to make it look as realistic as possible, Johnston had the Rocketeer stunt performers suspended by cables under a helicopter that flew at speeds of up to 90 mph (145 kph). The effects technicians rigged the jetpack to emit real fire trails and the Rocketeer costume had to be insulated against the open flames. These alterations to the costume and jetpack weighed an additional 50 lbs (23 kg), making the flying scenes that much more demanding for the performers. Costume designer Marilyn Vance-Straker created 40 versions of the Rocketeer jacket, and each one had a different function. One version had a panel with a parachute inside that was needed for a scene where the stunt performer does a 100 ft (30 m) freefall.

▶ Stunt performers were suspended from invisible wires to create the illusion of flight.

Animated Classics Come to Life

The rich legacy of Disney's animated classics inspires new live-action epics that transport animated characters into the realm of reality.

▲ In Disney's 1951 animated feature, Alice finds the experience intriguing as she slowly floats down the rabbit hole toward Wonderland.

Tim Burton's *Alice in Wonderland* (2010) tumbles back down the rabbit hole to a world Alice first entered as a child, where she embarks on a journey to discover her true identity. The wildly imaginative characters of Lewis Carroll's 1865 book and Walt Disney's 1951 animated adaptation naturally attracted the quirkily creative director. Burton believes Wonderland has remained viable because it taps into the things that people aren't aware of on a conscious level. The mixture of visual effects with CGI characters showcases Burton's vision in a richly detailed manner that is well-suited to the surreal Wonderland environment.

▼ In contrast to the animated version, the Alice of Tim Burton's 2010 adaptation is terrified as she falls down the rabbit hole.

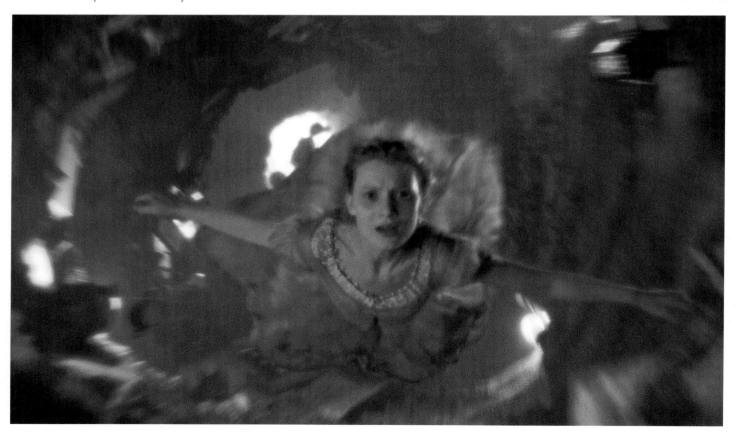

HISTORY MEETS FAIRY TALE

In one of most cherished moments in Walt Disney's animated classic *Cinderella* (1950), the Fairy Godmother transforms a hopeful serving girl's drab frock into a shimmering ball gown and puts sparkling glass slippers on her dainty feet. When it came to the 2015 live-action adaptation, three-time Academy Award®-winning costume designer Sandy Powell would play the Fairy Godmother in real life by creating a ball gown so beautiful, that it would seem almost to have been made by magic.

▲ The Fairy Godmother's spell transforms Cinderella into the belle of the ball in the original animated film.

▲ Fairy dust, or perhaps the talent of Academy Award®-winning Production Designer Dante Ferretti and his team, manifested Cinderella's golden carriage. It measured 10 ft (3.05 m) tall and 17 ft (5.2 m) in length.

"I had never considered directing a fairy tale, but I was captivated by the power of the story and thought I was in sync with the visual artistry." KENNETH BRANAGH (DIRECTOR)

▶ Powell started working on concepts for Cinderella's gowns two years before principal photography began. Cinderella's twelve-layer ballgown took 16 people more than 550 hours to create. Nine copies were used during production.

BOUND FOR THE BALL

One of the most spellbinding scenes in *Cinderella* (2015) is when the Fairy Godmother uses her magic to make sure that Ella shall go to the ball! With a flick of her wand, a pumpkin is transformed into a magnificent golden carriage. The carriage prop was decorated with gold leaf and weighed two tons (1,814 kg). Four mice are turned into horses, a goose becomes the coachman, and two lizards turn into footmen! The magic may only last until midnight, but Ella's happy memories of the ball will last forever.

▲ Piglet, Pooh, and friends call their now-adult human friend Christopher Robin back to the essence and joy of his childhood.

Of Teddy Bears and Wooden Boys

The promise of a favorite toy coming to life is the stuff animated dreams are made of ... and the subject of dreams come true in Disney's reimagined classics.

▲ Christopher Robin (Ewan McGregor) and Pooh (voiced by Jim Cummings) make up for long-lost time together in the live-action film.

A grown man is reunited with Pooh and other well-loved childhood friends in his time of need, as shown in *Christopher Robin* (2018). Their tale is a tuneful reunion with new original songs provided by Richard M. Sherman, half of the legendary brotherly duo that wrote most of the music for Walt Disney's original *Winnie the Pooh* projects. The timeless furry friends pick up from where they were shelved in Christopher's childhood past to show the adult how to reconnect with joy and wonder, and how to be a more present parent to his own child.

"I always get to where I'm going by walking away from where I've been." WINNIE THE POOH

◄ Christopher, Evelyn (Hayley Atwell), and Madeline (Bronte Carmichael) regroup as a family, with the help of some old friends.

Geppetto (Tom Hanks) puts the finishing touches on his beloved Pinocchio puppet, not knowing he will be a string-free son to him some day.

While he is part of Stromboli's show, Pinocchio is befriended by kindhearted puppeteer Fabiana (Kyanne Lamaya).

"The yearning of Geppetto, wanting to be a part of something bigger than himself, a part of a family, that was the whole bit."

TOM HANKS (GEPPETTO)

▲ Puppeteer Stromboli (Giuseppe Battiston) may be a gracious host onstage, but has an entirely different personality backstage.

▼ The Coachman (Luke Evans) seems like a great guy welcoming children to a great place, but the truth reveals itself in a very daunting and donkey-esque way for some in *Pinocchio*.

WISHING UPON A STAR

Geppetto has brought joy to others through decades of his woodworking magic, and at last it's his time to find his own happiness through his art in *Pinocchio* (2022). Bringing a wooden boy to life in traditional animation was a beautiful artistic journey in the original Disney film, but digitally carving the puppet for the live-action realm meant heightened challenges, such as wood grain needing to move like human skin. While much of the live-action film follows the storyline of the animated version, a few notable changes give the tale a new twist, such as the Blue Fairy singing "When You Wish Upon a Star," instead of Jiminy Cricket, and Pleasure Island being fraught with more modern temptations and challenges for the young guests who visit. New characters in the form of puppeteer Fabiana, ballerina puppet Sabina, and Sofia the seagull also appear in the 2022 film. Yet no matter how many updates the story of Pinocchio has, at its core it remains a strong lesson in honesty and being true to oneself.

Emanating Evil

These antagonists are even more fun to watch as they bring their bad-hearted schemes to big screen reality.

▲ Inspiration for Maleficent's costume came from the designs of legendary animator Marc Davis in Walt Disney's *Sleeping Beauty*.

The thrilling threat of Disney villains has captivated generation after generation of movie-goers in both animated and live-action mediums. The element of fantastic menace that fictional villains emit, both visually and thematically, makes them magnetic for audiences who wonder what these daring characters will try to get away with and how they will learn an undoubtedly important lesson—and in some moments, how they do it all while donning fascinating fashion.

▼ Angelina Jolie plays a vision of vileness as Maleficent, and not a typical godmother, as Aurora (Elle Fanning) comes to discover.

VILE VILLAINS

A fresh take on a fairy tale explores the untold story of Disney's most iconic villain from *Sleeping Beauty* (1959). The saga of *Maleficent* (2014) uncovers the betrayal that led to her pure heart turning to stone. The filmmakers wanted the evil fairy to have an element of fantasy and an unreal quality about her, but also to be grounded in reality. Maleficent's uniquely wicked style involved the talents of Oscar®-winning actress Angelina Jolie, as well as a team of artists and designers. Costume designer Anna B. Sheppard drew upon the work of Maleficent's original animator, Marc Davis, to create the flowing cape, high collar, and iconic horns of her dramatic costume. Producer and animation veteran Don Hahn believes that as storytellers, the filmmakers are called to reinvent these ancient stories, which is exactly what Walt did in his animated features and Disney continues to do in its live-action films. *Maleficent: Mistress of Evil* (2019) delves even deeper into the complex relationship between Aurora and Maleficent.

FURIOUS FASHION

The origin story of classic *One Hundred and One Dalmatians* villain Cruella De Vil reaches back to the youth of Estella (Emma Stone), whose creative mindset, hard-knock life, and chance meetings blend into a world of couture and cruelty in *Cruella* (2021). Emerging from her tough youth in the 1970s London punk scene, Estella transforms herself into a sinister sensation with an eye for design and devilry—and a complicated history with Dalmatians. *Cruella* strutted fashionista flair on the red carpet to receive an Academy Award® for "Best Costume Design" to honor the real-life talents of costume designer Jenny Beavan.

▲ Animator Marc Davis brought Cruella De Vil to life in a most mesmerizing way for the 1961 animated film.

▲ Young designer Estella has great aspirations for her career in fashion ... but at what cost?

▼ Cruella may mask herself in the name of fashion, but her true darkness seeps through her powerful yet stylish presence for the cameras.

▲ Cruella's skirt doubles as a car cover and required great poise from actor Emma Stone in order to gracefully walk up the vehicle and swish the skirt into place.

Magic and Music

Disney magic works in both animated and live-action settings, as seen in reimaginings of time-tested favorite cinematic storytelling.

When *Beauty and the Beast* (2017) appeared in live-action, the movie embraced its animated predecessor's musicality with great gusto, adding four additional original songs created by the legendary team of Alan Menken and Sir Tim Rice. Filmed in and around London, the movie required 27 physical sets to be built at Shepperton Studios. These sets were also digitized into a software system to support lighting and camera work that needed to incorporate both live actors and computer-generated characters and effects. Villeneuve, the village in which Belle lives in the retelling, was one such set built, and it is named after Gabrielle-Suzanne Barbot de Villeneuve,

▲ The ballroom scene portrays a whirlwind of romantic choreography between Belle (Emma Watson) and the Beast (Dan Stevens), in the live-action adaptation of the studio's animated classic.

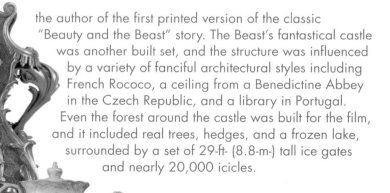

the author of the first printed version of the classic "Beauty and the Beast" story. The Beast's fantastical castle was another built set, and the structure was influenced by a variety of fanciful architectural styles including French Rococo, a ceiling from a Benedictine Abbey in the Czech Republic, and a library in Portugal. Even the forest around the castle was built for the film, and it included real trees, hedges, and a frozen lake, surrounded by a set of 29-ft- (8.8-m-) tall ice gates and nearly 20,000 icicles.

◄ The castle staff are alive and well in their sentient serving ware, time piece, and furnishing forms.

◀ The relationship of Dalia (Nasim Pedrad) and Jasmine (Naomi Scott) adds another level of connection and communication to the tale of *Aladdin*.

▶ Aladdin (Mena Massoud) and Jafar (Marwan Kenzari) make their acquaintances.

"This is a musical in its purest traditional form, and I liked the challenge."
GUY RITCHIE (DIRECTOR)

LARGER THAN LIFE

The Genie continues to provide laughter and wish-granting when he is freed from his lamp in the live-action *Aladdin* (2019). To find the perfect Jasmine and Aladdin, filmmakers spent more than a year casting the parts, auditioning 2,000 actors around the globe in the process. With the inclusion of new character Dalia in the story, audiences were granted a chance to learn more about Jasmine's perspective, as she verbalizes it to her handmaiden. The audience also sees deeper into Jafar's character, as this film reveals that his backstory is not unlike Aladdin's, with Jafar also being an orphan who must find his own way in the world. A musical lover's wish come true, the "Prince Ali" song sequence took five days and seven cameras to film, 250 dancers and 200 extras, and some 37,000 flowers to attach to the golden camel float—which itself took 15 model-makers three weeks to construct.

▲ Aladdin, in his Prince Ali persona, talks about experiencing the greater world with Princess Jasmine.

From Battleground to the Deep Blue

Characters with inner strength and magic come alive in epic scale and environments.

▲ Hua Mulan (Liu Yifei) is dressed and ready to meet with a matchmaker.

Although Mulan, Ariel, and Peter Pan came to animated cinematic life over the course of more than 40 years, their classic stories of bravery and belief in themselves are timelessly inspiring. Modern audiences have the fortune to be part of their worlds in both animated and live-action experiences.

HIDDEN HONOR

The power of a warrior shines through the darkness of war in the live-action film *Mulan* (2020), based on the Chinese poem "Ballad of Mulan." For the grand-scale production, large battle scenes required a massive artillery to be amassed: approximately 4,000 weapon props were crafted, including Mulan's father's detailed sword, which was made of bronze and steel with the words "Loyal Brave True" etched onto the blade. That vital prop also had an alternative version cast in lightweight rubber and carbon fiber that weighed a mere 11 oz (300 g), for ease of on-camera sword-fighting by Mulan.

▲ The design of the Emperor's Room was based on ancient buildings that still exist, but made grander and more golden to elevate the presence of the Emperor in both the eyes of Mulan and the audience.

◄ Mulan wields an impressive sword and inner warrior spirit.

THE WISDOM OF YOUTH

Growing up is hard to do, and not something Wendy Darling thinks she is ready to do as audiences first meet her in *Peter Pan & Wendy* (2023). When her youthful wish to spend time with her storybook friend Peter Pan comes true, Wendy goes on the adventure of a lifetime with her brothers Michael and John. She returns to the real world with a whole new perspective on what her future may hold, regardless of whether or not she encounters real-world foes reminiscent of Captain Hook.

▲ Peter Pan (Alexander Molony) and Wendy (Ever Anderson) hide out in Peter's room in the Lost Boys' house.

▶ Michael (Jacobi Jupe) and John Darling (Joshua Pickering) partake in swash-buckling, sword-play-fighting, brotherly fun.

GROUNDED ADVENTURE

The spirited young mermaid Ariel has always been fascinated with what happens above sea level, and the live-action reimagining of her classic story adds another level of reality to her tale. *The Little Mermaid* (2023) reprises favorite songs as it takes audiences along with Ariel, who makes her way to dry land by striking a deal with the villainous sea witch Ursula. After encountering life in the human world, Ariel has to ultimately balance her deep curiosity for all things human against the cost of her bargain with Ursula, putting her life and her father King Triton's domain at risk.

▲ Prince Eric (Jonah Hauer-King) realizes Ariel (Halle Bailey) is the person who saved him after he drifted unconscious deep underwater.

◀ Eric and Ariel examine a map of the human world in his castle, as he describes different locations and tells Ariel about his voyages.

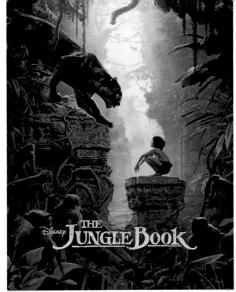

▲ Creating a world full of CG animals earned the filmmakers an Academy Award® for Best Visual Effects.

◄ Mowgli and Baloo croon their song "The Bare Necessities" amidst a leafy paradise in *The Jungle Book*.

Animal-Based Adventures

A new level of screen magic emerges when real and realistic animals portray classic animated Disney roles.

◄ The live canine stars of *101 Dalmatians* had their own 2,000 sq ft (186 sq m) climate-controlled residence at the Shepperton Studios in London.

T*he Jungle Book* (2016) finds Mowgli, Bagheera, and Baloo together again as the trusting trio at the heart of the original story and 1967 film, with moments of song to highlight the energy and fun of their friendship. In this re-telling, the storybook opening is more dimensional than the earlier film, the threat of Shere Khan feels stronger, and Kaa has the most mesmerizing personality shift, and is now a female-voiced character.

POOCH POWER
Cuteness abounds in *101 Dalmatians* (1996), which was filmed with a blend of animatronic and live dogs in and around London, with lots of bark-filled fun throughout seven sound stages at Shepperton Studios. The high-fashion sensibility of Cruella De Vil was worn well by Glenn Close as she was outfitted by her trusted Broadway collaborator, costume designer Anthony Powell. The pups came back to the big screen in *102*

► Cruella is fresh out of prison in *102 Dalmatians*, but her not-so-reformed behavior suggests that perhaps a trip to obedience school is in order.

Dalmatians (2000) when the offspring of Dipstick, one of the original 101, are now in Cruella's sights.

▲ Young Simba, Timon, and Pumbaa find joy in following the musically manifested motto "Hakuna Matata" and having no worries.

▶ Simba and Nala feel the love as they explore the beauty of the savanna.

A FATHER'S PRIDE LANDS

The rise of Simba to his royal standing is vividly portrayed in *The Lion King* (2019). Audiences gave a roaring response to the beauty of Africa, Simba's ever-entertaining kinship with Timon and Pumbaa, and the robust soundtrack that gathers the talents of Sir Elton John, Sir Tim Rice, and Beyoncé, as well as the song "He Lives in You" from the Broadway production.

A TAIL OF TWO WORLDS

When a sheltered and civilized Cocker Spaniel is cast out of her cushioned life, she is lucky to encounter a street-smart mutt to show her the lay of the land. In *Lady and the Tramp* (2019), the leading canines were played by well-bred Rose and rescue hound Monte, who spent three days filming the memorable spaghetti-eating scene with the taste of sugar-free, uncolored licorice strings, simmered in chicken broth, on their pup prop plates.

▼ The courting canines enjoy dinner for two, with strings attached, in *Lady and the Tramp.*

From Parks to Screens: A Pirate's Life

Inspired by the classic Disneyland Park attraction, *Pirates of the Caribbean: The Curse of the Black Pearl* launched a mighty series of swashbuckling adventure films.

▲ Coin props from the movies

When producer Jerry Bruckheimer asked Gore Verbinski to direct *Pirates of the Caribbean: The Curse of the Black Pearl* (2003) Gore said he felt as excited as a nine-year-old boy. That enthusiasm was infectious, with actor Johnny Depp also hearkening back to his childhood dreams to play a pirate.

The now-iconic costume of offbeat pirate Captain Jack Sparrow helped Depp bring the character to life. Working with costume designer Penny Rose, Depp was outfitted with an array of period costuming, including hats, boots, belts, and a pistol (a 1760 antique from a London gun maker). Depp spent only 45 minutes at the mirror before finding Jack Sparrow's perfect look. He selected the trinkets to wear in his hair and the signature pirate hat was an instinctive choice—he was presented with seven hats and immediately chose the leather tricorn.

◀ Captain Jack Sparrow (Johnny Depp) wields his sword, an antique from the 18th century.

▶ Jack's magical compass doesn't point north, but to the thing he wants most. A magnet was added to the compass so that it would behave accordingly.

SWASHBUCKLING SEQUELS

The task of reconvening exactly the same creative and technical teams for a sequel was a big concern, and the decision was made to shoot the next two installments to complete an initial trilogy, *Dead Man's Chest* (2006) and *At World's End* (2007) simultaneously. The fourth film, *Pirates of the Caribbean: On Stranger Tides* (2011) was filmed in 3D to give audiences a greater sense of immersion. *Pirates of the Caribbean: Dead Men Tell No Tales* (2017) is a tale in which Jack must find the Trident of Poseidon, known for giving its owner mystical power over the sea.

DEAD MAN'S CHEST

In *Pirates of the Caribbean: Dead Man's Chest*, Captain Jack Sparrow finds himself once again in a life-or-death scenario, with the ruler of the ocean depths, Davy Jones in the mix. Jack visits the mysterious Tia Dalma, who tells Jack he must find the fabled Dead Man's Chest that contains Davy Jones' heart in order to save his own life. Many others are ruthlessly seeking this piratical object of desire as well, and it takes quite a beating throughout the film. Johnny Depp had to act as though he were carrying a heavy iron chest, although the stunt version of the iconic prop was in fact made of rubber. Prop master Kris Peck noted that the goal was to make the mystical chest appear unbreakable, like a cast-iron skillet, while featuring detailing of the film's themes.

An antique, hardware finish makes the chest look like it is from the long-ago world of the film.

The stunt prop chest was made to look heavy, as if made of cast-iron, but is actually flexible and light so that it could withstand the repeated manhandling during filming.

Lock can be opened by a special double-pronged key.

Lock design resembles a heart when closed and a crab when open.

Marine life motifs resemble the Kraken and tentacles on Davy Jones' face.

▶ The location shoot for *The Curse of the Black Pearl* included at least 20 different islands, 3 large pirate ships, and 900 pieces of clothing.

Expanded Adventures

The creative spirit of Disney's theme park experiences inspires continued fun when the adventure leaps from parks to screens.

A few of the films inspired by favorite Disney Park experiences include a television movie based on The Twilight Zone Tower of Terror attraction from 1997, a feature loosely inspired by the Mission to Mars attraction through Disney's Touchstone film banner in 2000, and a 2002 feature that portrays what might happen if the real-life members of the Country Bear Jamboree show regrouped. One of the most popular projects takes audiences on a feature-length *Jungle Cruise* (2021), based on its namesake attraction.

ACTION AFLOAT

Jungle Cruise follows scientist Dr. Lily Houghton and her brother MacGregor as they hop on a small Amazon riverboat in search of the Tree of Life, racing against another expedition and cursed conquistadors from centuries past to find it. With a bit more fast-paced action than guests experience on the real-life attraction in Disney Parks, the explorers' adventures are wrought with twists, turns, and a generous supply of puns floated by the boat's captain, Frank Wolff.

▲ Frank Wolff strums away on the Vihuela.

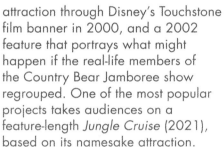

◄ Frank Wolff (Dwayne Johnson) and Dr. Lily Houghton (Emily Blunt) are riverbound in *Jungle Cruise*.

► Skipper Frank Wolff and MacGregor Houghton (Jack Whitehall) have a chat about the river cruise logistics.

◄ Beautiful Porto Velho is the launching point for *Jungle Cruise*.

"First of all, let me congratulate you on your excellent choice of skipper." FRANK WOLFF

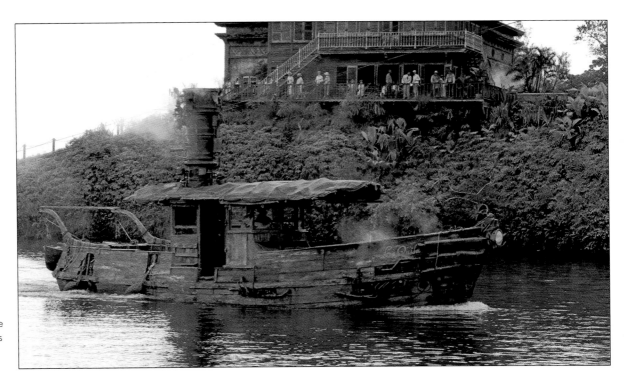

► It may not look like much, but *La Quila* is the vessel of success in *Jungle Cruise*.

The Wonderful World of Television

Disney entertainment is welcomed on the small screen in living rooms and handheld devices all over the world.

▲ Walt changed the name of his anthology series to *Walt Disney's Wonderful World of Color* in 1961, and sales of color televisions soared.

Walt Disney was the first major Hollywood producer to enter the world of television with his *One Hour in Wonderland* special in 1950. In 1954, he launched a one-hour weekly anthology series on ABC, entitled *Disneyland*. The show was an instant hit, especially with its "Davy Crockett" episodes about the real-life frontiersman, which started a U.S.-wide "Crockett" craze. Under various titles, the primetime series— perhaps best known as *The Wonderful World of Disney*—was broadcast for 29 consecutive seasons, airing on all of the three major networks at the time. In 1955, Walt debuted the ground-breaking *Mickey Mouse Club*, one of the most famous children's shows in television history. The unique daily variety show featured a talented group of young Disney discoveries called the Mouseketeers. Other revivals have appeared through the decades, some of which launched careers of future stars including Britney Spears, Christina Aguilera, and Ryan Gosling.

TEEN SPIRIT

In the early 21st century, Disney Channel and Disney XD became the go-to destinations for hit comedy series that reflected young people's everyday lives

◀ Walt Disney surrounded by some of the *Mickey Mouse Club* cast.

▶ Miley Cyrus rocks out as Hannah Montana.

"... the ideas, the knowledge and the emotions that come through the television screen in our living rooms will most certainly shape the course of the future for ourselves and our children." WALT DISNEY

such as *Even Stevens, That's So Raven, Austin & Ally, Wizards of Waverly Place, Kickin' It, Liv & Maddie,* and *The Suite Life of Zack & Cody,* to name a few. Premiering in 2001, *Lizzie McGuire* (title character played by Hilary Duff) portrayed a teen trying to fit in at school, with animated sequences illustrating her inner thoughts. When *Hannah Montana* debuted in 2006, it became a worldwide phenomenon. Playing an average teen by day and a superstar by night, Miley Cyrus skyrocketed to stardom. These channels also helped launch the music careers of stars such as Demi Lovato and the Jonas Brothers.

CLASS ACT

Also debuting in 2006 and creating a global sensation was *High School Musical,* a Disney Channel Original Movie, or DCOM. A combination of teen romance and musical theater, the movie, starring Zac Efron and Vanessa Hudgens, was renowned for its elaborate dance routines. *High School Musical 2* made its debut on Disney Channel in 2007 as the most watched single piece of programming in cable history as of that moment in time. *High School Musical 3: Senior Year* was theatrically released in 2008.

▲ Go Wildcats! Student voices ring out in song in *High School Musical.*

MIND THE CHILDREN

Descendants (2015) was a wickedly popular DCOM, following the lives of the teenage offspring of Jafar, Cruella De Vil, Maleficent, and the Evil Queen. Audiences were so bewitched that they also enjoyed two sequels plus a short-form computer-animated series, *Descendants: Wicked World* (2015).

▲ Classic Disney villains Jafar (Maz Jobrani), Evil Queen (Kathy Najimy), Maleficent (Kristin Chenoweth), and Cruella De Vil (Wendy Raquel Robinson) have their hands full when they become parents of teenagers in *Descendants.*

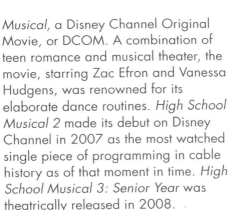

► Teen spirit runs strong in the spawn of famous Disney villains. It emanates from these strong-willed characters in *Descendants.*

Muppet Magic

The lovable characters created by Jim Henson have entertained their way into the hearts of fans since the 1970s, and The Muppets Studio has expanded those fuzzy feelings to broader audiences in more recent times.

▲ Mini-Muppets brought a whole new level of cuteness to the world in *Muppet Babies* mode.

When Jim Henson introduced Kermit the Frog on *Sam and Friends*, a Washington D.C.-based television show in 1955, it may have been hard to imagine that an entire legacy could be crafted out of an old coat and a ping-pong ball cut in half. While Kermit can attest to the fact that "it's not easy being green," clearly his appearance on *Sesame Street* alongside other Henson characters laid a path for his fellow Muppets to follow their way to screens of all sizes, for generations to come.

UNDER THE STAGE LIGHTS

Kermit and other mainstay Muppets got their first big break on *The Muppet Show*, a weekly primetime broadcast series that ran from 1976 to 1981. The premise of *The Muppet Show* was a sketch comedy show seen from multiple production perspectives including onstage skits, musical numbers, backstage antics, and audience heckling. The regular cast included Kermit the Frog, Miss Piggy, Fozzie Bear, Gonzo, Scooter, Sam the Eagle, the Swedish Chef, the band The Electric Mayhem, plus Statler and Waldorf on the balcony. They were joined by a top-notch list of featured *human* celebrities who were very special guests on the show. *Muppets Tonight* (1996) continued the fun of the original show but shifted from a theater-based to a broadcast show premise set in the KMUP studios. *the Muppets* (2015) introduced another perspective on the lives of Miss Piggy, Kermit, and a cast of familiar characters, by following them on set for the production of the *Up Late with Miss Piggy* talk show. In *The Muppets Mayhem* (2023), audiences discovered the fantastical origins of the beloved Muppet house band, The Electric Mayhem, as they recorded their first studio album after 45 years of rocking out.

SMALL PACKAGES

Muppet Babies have been cast in both traditionally animated (1984) and computer-generated versions (2018). The prequel-like concept was conceived in a scene in the film *The Muppets Take Manhattan* (1984), when Miss Piggy wonders what she and her "Kermie" would have been like together as toddlers.

◀ Kermit, Fozzie, Gonzo, and a dangling Rizzo are riding high with a crow's-nest view of the big, blue wet thing in the feature film *Muppet Treasure Island* (1996).

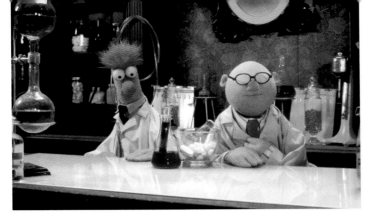

OF CAPERS AND CAROLS

The Muppets have brought their energy to feature-length productions eight times, starting with *The Muppet Movie* in 1979. The film is both an origin story and a road picture, with Kermit the Frog on a cross-country drive to find his place in show business, discovering like-minded companions along the way. "The Rainbow Connection" was a touching musical performance by Kermit in this film, which went on to achieve top hit status on radio playlists. In *The Muppet Christmas Carol* (1992), director Brian Henson ambitiously sought to cast Kermit the Frog walking in full-frame as a true puppet, which had never before been filmed. The mighty cinematic effort was successfully achieved with a rolling barrel mechanism under Kermit's webbed feet. Other feature films include the more recent *The Muppets* (2011) and *Muppets Most Wanted* (2014). The Muppets have also headlined more than two dozen television movies and specials, including an eerie Disney+ project that was simply to die for: *Muppets Haunted Mansion* (2021).

▲ "Muppets Labs" was one of the most-loved recurring sketches on *The Muppet Show*, featuring Beaker, Dr. Bunsen Honeydew, and a whole lot of explosive science.

▲ The musical stylings of The Electric Mayhem are crafted by the combined talents of Dr. Teeth on vocals and keys, Animal pounding on drums, Janice on vocals and strumming lead guitar, Floyd Pepper on vocals and grooving bass, Lips on Trumpet, and Zoot on the smooth saxophone.

▲ In *Muppets Haunted Mansion*, Gonzo and Pepé are tasked with spending Halloween night in the scariest place on Earth—The Haunted Mansion. The creative teams partnered with Walt Disney Imagineering to capture all the details from the grim, grinning Disney attraction, including designing Muppet versions of the iconic wallpapers and decor.

▶ Gonzo, Fozzie, Kermit, Miss Piggy, Rowlf, and Scooter are decked out and ready to entertain in *Muppets Most Wanted*.

"*I think what I want Disneyland to be most of all is a happy place—a place where adults and children can experience together some of the wonders of life, of adventure, and feel better because of it.*" WALT DISNEY

Disney
Experiences

Attraction Posters

From Alice in Wonderland to the Matterhorn, the attractions of the Disney Theme Parks worldwide have inspired a dazzling variety of posters. As veteran Imagineer Marty Sklar said, "The posters are enticing pieces of theater that give the audience previews of what's to come." Often placed at the main entrance—like in a cinema lobby—these beautifully designed placards tantalize with stylized graphics and lively slogans. Every day, tens of thousands of guests pass the Disney Theme Park posters, which provide an artful experience in visual adventure.

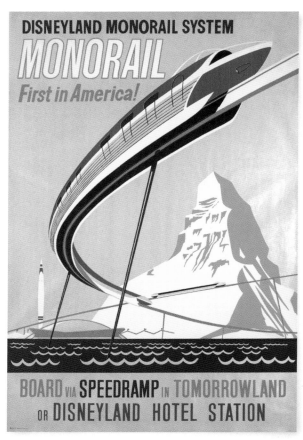

MONORAIL, DISNEYLAND (1959)
Artist Paul Hartley used imagery of the first "E Ticket" attractions—Matterhorn Mountain and the Monorail—in this classic Disneyland Park poster.

LE CHATEAU DE LA BELLE AU BOIS DORMANT, DISNEYLAND PARIS (1992)
Designed by Disney artists Tracy Trinast and Tom Morris, this poster sets the tone for Disneyland Paris, with the iconic image of one of the most fanciful of the Disney castles.

SOARIN' OVER CALIFORNIA, DISNEY CALIFORNIA ADVENTURE (2001)
This poster, developed by Greg Maletic, gives guests a taste of an exciting attraction—a simulated glider ride over California's scenic vistas.

BIG THUNDER MOUNTAIN RAILROAD, DISNEYLAND (1977) This poster concept for the Frontierland classic by Jim Michaelson graphically captures the wildness of the runaway train coaster-like attraction.

WORLD BAZAAR, TOKYO DISNEYLAND (2002) Will Eyerman's poster, adapted from the original 1983 poster by Rudy Lord and Greg Paul, translates the idealized vision of Victorian Americana for an international audience.

ORBITRON—MACHINES VOLANTES, DISNEYLAND PARIS (1992) Tim Delaney and Jim Michaelson capture the pulp-science fiction tone of the works of H. G. Wells and Jules Verne, with their larger-than-life illustrations.

20,000 LEAGUES UNDER THE SEA EXHIBIT, DISNEYLAND (1955) Artist Bjorn Aronson employed powerful graphics for his poster for this exhibit—a display of the original sets and menacing giant squid used in 20,000 Leagues Under the Sea (1954).

The Art of Imagineering

Walt Disney and his team were always exploring and experimenting. He called it Imagineering— a combination of imagination and engineering. Walt Disney Imagineering (WDI) comprises Imagineers, who design and build Disney Parks and other entertainment venues. It was founded on December 16, 1952, under the name WED (Walter Elias Disney) Enterprises. From writers and architects, to artists and beyond, the Imagineers employ a variety of skills in the Disney tradition of artistry and technical innovation. Many of their stories can be seen and read about in the Disney+ documentary and companion book, *The Imagineering Story*, crafted by Leslie Iwerks.

ONE LITTLE SPARK
Herb Ryman, one of the first Imagineers, working on concept art for Disneyland Paris. Ryman worked with Walt one historic weekend in 1953 to create the first visualization of Disneyland Park.

PRESIDENTIAL SCULPTOR
Blaine Gibson, one of Imagineering's master sculptors, sculpts Jimmy Carter in 1976 for the Hall of Presidents at Magic Kingdom Park in Walt Disney World Resort. Since Walt Disney World opened in 1971, an *Audio-Animatronics*® figure has been made of the likeness of each newly elected U.S. President.

YO HO, YO HO!
Xavier "X" Atencio, writer and lyricist for the Pirates of the Caribbean attraction, works on the "barker bird" that once welcomed guests to the attraction at Walt Disney World Resort.

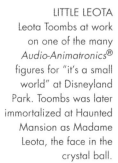

LITTLE LEOTA
Leota Toombs at work on one of the many *Audio-Animatronics*® figures for "it's a small world" at Disneyland Park. Toombs was later immortalized at Haunted Mansion as Madame Leota, the face in the crystal ball.

DOING THE IMPOSSIBLE
Bill Justice studies reference actors for programming the Pirates of the Caribbean *Audio-Animatronics*® figures.

FANTASY COMES TO LIFE
Harriet Burns at work in 1971 on the Mickey Mouse Revue, Magic Kingdom, Walt Disney World. One of Walt's biggest dreams when creating Disneyland was to build a place where his animated characters could interact with their fans.

FINE ART AND ARTISANS
Great attention to detail is needed to realize Disney attractions. It requires skilled artists, such as the painters seen here creating the ceiling mural in Magellan's restaurant at Mediterranean Harbor, Tokyo DisneySea.

TACTILE DREAMING
Walt Disney Imagineering comprises a variety of disciplines to create authentic environments. Lynne Itamura, Ellen Guevara, and Kyle Barnes work in the Interiors Department, and are responsible for decorating parks with wallpaper, carpet, and other materials.

ADORNING THE CASTLE
Imagineers play a vital role in planning the celebrations held at Disney Parks. Here, Owen Yoshino designs commemorative decorations for the 50th anniversary of Disneyland Park in 2005.

MINIATURE WORLD
When designing new attractions, shops, and eateries, Imagineers construct scale models. This is Claude Coats with the model of the Village Inn Restaurant (later Red Rose Taverne), New Fantasyland, Disneyland in 1983.

PITCHING THE PARK
Peter Ellenshaw created this full color aerial view of Walt's burgeoning Magic Kingdom in 1954. The legendary Disney artist painted his expansive rendering on a 4 x 8 ft (1.2 x 2.4 m) storyboard—overpainted with phosphorescent paint for a nighttime effect—for Walt to present on his *Disneyland* television series.

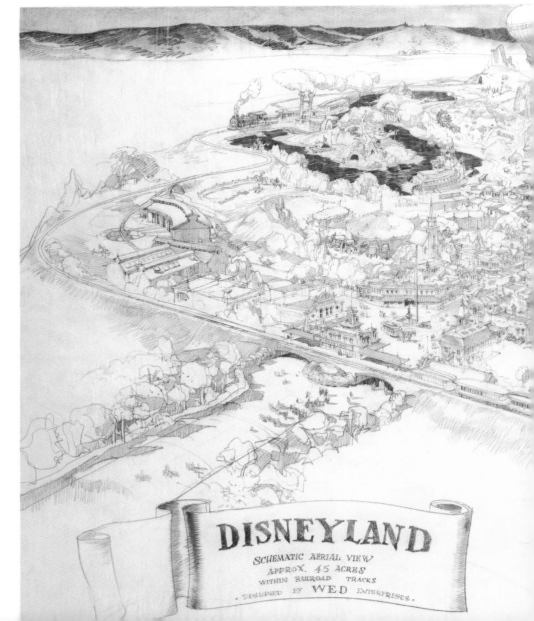

DISNEYLAND

SCHEMATIC AERIAL VIEW
APPROX. 45 ACRES
WITHIN RAILROAD TRACKS
DESIGNED BY WED ENTERPRISES

Mapping a Magic Kingdom

There had never been anything like the "magical little park" Walt had been dreaming up since at least the late 1930s. As with his filmed productions, Walt knew that visualization was the optimal way to both develop and share concepts, especially one as revolutionary as the park Walt would come to call "Disneyland" (a name first used for the project in 1952). Beyond even castles, riverboats, and rocket ships, Walt's groundbreaking layout encompassed four themed "lands" radiating out from a central hub. The great showman knew his vision had to be mapped out in detail to gain the financial support needed to make his dream a reality.

THE FIRST LOOK
Created under the direct supervision of Walt Disney over the weekend of September 23, 1953, this pencil concept sketch by artist Herb Ryman is the first true visualization of what is now recognized as Disneyland Park.

Walt Disney's Magic Kingdom

A revolutionary family entertainment never seen before, Walt Disney's Disneyland Park opened up the whole Disney experience to guests from all over the world.

▲ 1965 First Disneyland Ambassador Julie Reihm, Walt, and Imagineer John Hench review a model for the new Plaza Inn during the park's "Tencennial" celebration.

The original Disney Park created by Walt Disney, Disneyland Park, is such a big part of the world's collective culture that it is easy to forget that this concept in family entertainment was revolutionary. Walt felt that visitors to the Studio should have something to see besides artists sitting at desks in small rooms. It was on "Daddy's Day"—the Saturdays when he took his two daughters to small local amusement parks—that inspiration struck. Walt was often left sitting on the bench eating peanuts while his daughters rode the merry-go-round and had all the fun—and he took this time to dream. But Walt dreamed of something more than just another amusement park and his idea was something entirely new—an all-encompassing environment that would be designed around themes. It would be clean, orderly, and welcoming, and a three-dimensional experience of Disney characters, stories, concepts, and fun. This "magical little park," as Walt referred to his brainchild, would be a *theme park*.

A NEW ENTERTAINMENT

As soon as Walt began shaping the early visions for Disneyland Park, he invited several of his most versatile animators and art directors to apply the principles of filmmaking to the three-dimensional world he was creating. But it was Walt himself who innovated the idea. Unlike other amusement parks, fairs, or museums of a single entrance, his would channel guests down Main Street, U.S.A., into various Disney "realms" of fantasy, including the history of the U.S., and the optimistic promise of the future, all radiating from a central hub.

WALT'S LEGACY

Disneyland Park opened on July 17, 1955, presenting 18 major attractions on its opening day, including the now-classic Jungle Cruise, Autopia, and Mark Twain Riverboat. The Imagineers who uphold Walt's creative legacy have continued to pioneer extraordinary attractions (never "rides") that can only be experienced by "guests" (never "customers") at Disneyland and other Disney Parks—because, as Walt pledged, "Disneyland will never be completed, it will … grow as long as there is imagination left in the world."

◄ Two iconic symbols of Disneyland Park: Sleeping Beauty Castle and Mickey Mouse.

▲ The 105-ft-long (32 m) Mark Twain Riverboat was the first paddle wheeler constructed in the U.S. in 50 years.

◄ 1959 saw the introduction of three innovative attractions: Matterhorn Bobsleds, Submarine Voyage, and the Monorail.

"We believed in our idea—a family park where parents and children could have fun together." WALT DISNEY

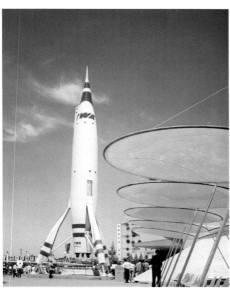

▲ Since 1955, Tomorrowland has offered futuristic adventures, such as this iconic early attraction, Rocket to the Moon (1955–1961).

▼ Disney California Adventure Park opened in 2001 as part of the Disneyland Resort. The park's Sun Wheel attraction later became Mickey's Fun Wheel (shown here), and is now the Pixar Pal-A-Round.

▲ A host of Disney characters—headed by Mickey Mouse and his pals—may be seen greeting guests throughout Disneyland Park.

A New Kind of World

In Florida, Walt had found a space big enough to encapsulate his dreams, ideas, and imagination.

▲ With then-Governor of Florida, W. Haydon Burns, Walt and Roy Disney announce the project that would become Walt Disney World Resort.

After the success of Disneyland Park in California, Walt Disney began to consider a new Disney project. As early as 1959 he was looking at options for a new "destination development" in locations east of the Mississippi River, including Florida. Many factors were considered, such as land cost, population density, and accessibility. The warm climate in Florida seemed the best for year-round operation, and by 1964, Disney agents began to secure what would become a land parcel near Orlando of more than 27,400 acres (11,088 ha) in total—twice the size of Manhattan Island. Walt declared that the "Florida Project" would be a whole Disney world of ideas and entertainment—a new, different kind of world.

PLANNING BEGINS

Walt and Roy announced their Florida plans publicly on November 15, 1965, but Walt Disney died suddenly, a year later, in December 1966. Roy, who was 73 years old,

> "There's enough land here to hold all the ideas and plans we can possibly imagine." WALT DISNEY

▲ Magic Kingdom Park is divided into six themed lands: Main Street, U.S.A., Adventureland, Tomorrowland, Fantasyland, Frontierland, and, unique to Florida, Liberty Square, home to the Hall of Presidents attraction.

▶ Roy O. Disney dedicates Walt Disney World Resort to the memory of his brother, Walt. Just two months later, on December 20, 1971, Roy passed away.

was ready to retire, but was determined to stay on the job long enough to see Walt's final project to its fruition. Led by Roy, the team that Walt had formed continued to dream, imagine, and plan. Construction began in 1969, and more than 8,000 construction workers labored around the clock so that Magic Kingdom Park could open in 1971. Sparkling lagoons and artificial beaches emerged where there had once been murky swamps and scrub pine forests. A state-of-the-art Monorail system was constructed, with the sleek Monorail trains even gliding directly through the A-frame of Disney's Contemporary Resort hotel.

A DREAM COME TRUE
Right on schedule—for in 1966 Walt Disney had told the press the new resort would open in five years—Magic Kingdom Park, the first of four theme parks, opened October 1, 1971. When he presided at the grand opening, Roy dedicated Walt Disney World Resort as a tribute to the philosophy and life of Walter Elias Disney. He insisted that the new resort be called Walt Disney World so that everyone would always know the dreamer behind the dream come true.

▲ Imagineer Herb Ryman's 1969 acrylic painting conveys the towering majesty and fanciful feel of the 189 ft (58 m) tall Cinderella Castle, the center of Magic Kingdom Park.

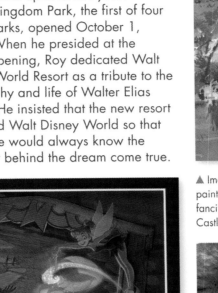

► Concept art by Nina Rae Vaughn of Mickey's PhilharMagic, a 3D film featuring Disney characters, at Fantasyland

▲ Guests can explore the bejeweled mines like Dopey does on the Seven Dwarfs Mine Train, which opened in 2014.

▲ Concept art of New Fantasyland by Greg Pro. The expansion was the largest in the history of Magic Kingdom Park, nearly doubling Fantasyland in size when it was completed in 2014.

► Slinky Dog Dash (opened in 2018) adds a twisty dash of fun to Toy Story Land at Disney's Hollywood Studios in Walt Disney World.

Slinky ® Dog © Just Play LLC

The Wonders of Nature

Disney created a special park to bring love and respect for animals closer to the human experience and heart.

▲ Set in an old train depot, Harambe Market welcomes guests to enjoy the food and feel of a vibrant Kenyan village.

I n creating Disney's Animal Kingdom Theme Park for Walt Disney World Resort in 1998, the Imagineers were confronted with a unique challenge. They had to devise a castle-like centerpiece in a realm where architecture is secondary to lush landscaping, blooming plants, and amazing animals (there are around 1,000 animals, representing 200 species) living in natural settings. The solution was an immense tree named the Tree of Life that would not only represent this one-of-a-kind kingdom, but also encompass all of nature and life itself. This extraordinary icon rises from Discovery Island.

▶ In this magnificent concept painting by Tom Gilleon, the artist imagined the Tree of Life—a vision of how powerfully the symbol expresses the intricate balance of nature.

FUN WITH MOVIES AND MOVING

The quintessential Disney theme park experience includes creative attractions, live shows, and cinematic adventures, and Animal Kingdom offers a herd of options for its guests to enjoy. A few examples include the 3D film *It's Tough to Be a Bug!*, which provides entertainment and education about fascinating insects of the world; the live musical show *Festival of the Lion King*; and the Kali River Rapids attraction, which welcomes riders to soak in the thrill of a rafting adventure.

CONSERVATION IS KEY

Honoring and caring for the planet, including all of its furred, feathered, and finned creatures, is central to the Animal Kingdom theme. Through discovery tours, educational shows, and interactive experiences—including petting animals such as pigs and goats at the Affection Section—human guests build deeper connections to their animal co-habitants of Earth and will hopefully take away joyful memories, along with an inspired desire to protect wilderness and wildlife around the world.

▲ The thrill of a speeding train ride and a glimpse of the Yeti deliver a mountain of fun on the Expedition Everest—Legend of the Forbidden Mountain attraction.

▶▼ Giraffes, hippos, and tigers are just a few of the animal residents that might be encountered when hiking on the Gorilla Falls Exploration Trail or experiencing the Kilimanjaro Safaris attraction.

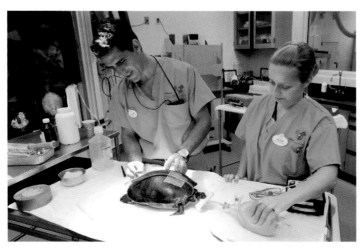

◀ Highly trained veterinarians provide care to special residents at the Conservation Station.

▶ Rafiki from *The Lion King* (1994) welcomes guests to Rafiki's Planet Watch.

Disney's Discovery Park

A celebration of human achievement and nations around the world, EPCOT builds on Walt Disney's innovative vision.

Celebrating the human spirit, imagination, and ingenuity, the 340-acre (137-ha) EPCOT at Walt Disney World Resort is divided into four distinct neighborhoods. World Discovery welcomes guests to enjoy stories about technology, science, and intergalactic adventures. World Showcase is a global gathering place for international experiences from architectural, cuisine, and cultural perspectives. World Nature invites guests to appreciate the beauty of the natural world, with experiences that celebrate both the land and water elements of our planet. World Celebration is a place that invites guests to connect with one another, and the greater world.

A NEW WAY OF LIVING

When dreaming of the place that was to be called EPCOT (Experimental Prototype Community of Tomorrow), Walt Disney envisioned a showcase for innovation, where cutting-edge technology could help develop new solutions for optimal living. Toward the end of his life, he became interested in the challenges presented by modern cities, from transportation to urban sprawl. Walt had pored over books on city planning, and with his experience in developing Disneyland Park and transit systems such as the Monorail, he believed that he and his Imagineers could come up with solutions. Uninterested in simply creating "another" Disneyland Park in Florida, Walt made a film in October

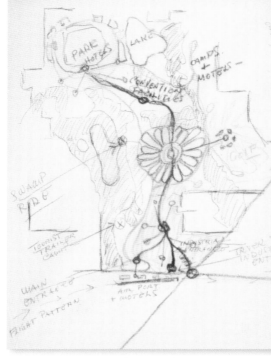

▲ At a 1966 meeting, Walt presented this hand-drawn sketch of the Florida property. This drawing remained the basic model for Walt Disney World Resort, which eventually included EPCOT, the theme park.

1966, which explained some of his ideas for a planned community. He wanted to build a place where people could live in an environment like no other. With the huge number of acres that Walt was accumulating in Florida, an ideal place for the concept was available within the project that would soon be known as Walt Disney World.

▼ "Project X" concept art painted by Herb Ryman of the transport center beneath the downtown center. Project X was the original working name for EPCOT.

▲ The symbol for all of EPCOT, the freestanding 18-floor geosphere Spaceship Earth stands 180 ft (55 m) high and is 165 ft (50 m) in diameter.

▲ Imagineers Terry Palmer and Berj Behesnilian work on the master model of EPCOT Center in 1980, adding finishing details to the plywood, paper, and cardboard model of Germany.

"EPCOT is ... an experimental prototype community that will always be in a state of becoming. It will never cease to be a living blueprint of the future." WALT DISNEY

▲ An early concept model shows a section of World Showcase, where guests can experience international cultures, wares, and cuisines on a promenade that surrounds a lagoon.

INNOVATIVE VISION

Walt Disney died in 1966, long before he and his artists could fully explore the preliminary concepts he had in mind. But the Imagineers carried on, inspired by their leader's vision. On October 1, 1978, Card Walker—CEO of Walt Disney Productions—revealed plans for EPCOT, a theme park inspired by Walt's philosophies. A groundbreaking ceremony was held one year later, and EPCOT Center opened on October 1, 1982. As Card expressed in the dedication, EPCOT is a place of joy, hope, and friendship and was inspired by Walt Disney's creative vision. It is a place where human achievements are celebrated through imagination, wonders of enterprise, and concepts of a future that promise new and exciting benefits.

▲ Elsa, Anna, and Olaf celebrate Summer Snow Day in the Frozen Ever After attraction at the Norway pavilion of World Showcase.

Disneyland Goes Global

The turrets of Cinderella Castle tower above Tokyo Bay, where a Magic Kingdom stands in tribute to Walt Disney's timeless vision.

▲ Located in Urayasu, Tokyo Disney Resort is home to two theme parks, Tokyo Disneyland and Tokyo DisneySea.

"May Tokyo Disneyland be an eternal source of joy, laughter, inspiration, and imagination to the peoples of the world." TOKYO DISNEYLAND DEDICATION, APRIL 15, 1983

Known as the Kingdom of Magic and Dreams to its Japanese guests, Tokyo Disney Resort opened its gates on April 15, 1983, bringing the magic of Disney-themed entertainment to Japan and establishing the first Disney theme park outside the United States. Tokyo Disney Resort is not only Japan's most popular family destination—it's also one of the most visited theme parks in the world.

THEME PARK PLANS
The history of Tokyo Disney Resort goes back a lot farther than 1983, with the idea of a Disney theme park in Japan originating in 1974. At that time, there were two Disney destinations: Disneyland Park in California and Walt Disney World Resort in Florida. The latter was barely three years old and consisted of a single park, Magic Kingdom Park.

It was at this point that plans for a Disney Park outside the continental U.S. began. In 1974, Keisei Electric Railway Co., Ltd., Mitsui & Co., Ltd., and Mitsui Fudosan Co., Ltd. sent an invitation under joint signature to Walt Disney Productions requesting that their executives visit Japan. In 1977, the name "Tokyo Disneyland" was officially announced, followed in 1980 by Japanese cast members

◄ Mickey and Minnie Mouse have been welcoming guests to Tokyo Disneyland since 1983.

▲ Festive parades, processions, and colorful festivals are a mainstay at the Magic Kingdom-style park.

▲ Cinderella Castle is home to the Grand Hall, where guests can view artworks that tell the story of the scullery maid-turned-princess.

▶ Meet the World attraction at Tomorrowland in Tokyo Disneyland was a show that explored Japan's heritage in a rotating theater.

being sent to Disneyland for training. In December of that year, ground was broken with a site dedication and the 1983 grand opening was set as their goal.

TOKYO DISNEYLAND TODAY

The tremendous popularity of Disney films and memorabilia in Japan made it a perfect site for the first non-U.S. Disney Park. The Japanese had long admired what had been achieved in California and Florida, and wanted many of the attractions from their Magic Kingdom-style parks recreated for Tokyo Disneyland. The park opened on schedule with more than 30 attractions in five themed lands, including World Bazaar (an adaptation of Main Street, U.S.A.) and Westernland. Today, the park's realms include Critter Country and Toontown. In 2001, Tokyo DisneySea, a 100-acre (40-ha) aquatic-themed park, opened next to Tokyo Disneyland. On entering and viewing a unique AquaSphere, guests can visit seven distinct themed ports— Mediterranean Harbor, Mysterious Island, Mermaid Lagoon, Arabian Coast, Lost River Delta, Port Discovery, and American Waterfront.

◀ The Fortress at Explorers' Landing stands as a golden landmark at Tokyo DisneySea, and the volcano on Mysterious Island adds another layer of intrigue to the setting.

▼ Guests explore a whole new level of the planet in Journey to the Center of the Earth on Mysterious Island at Tokyo DisneySea.

Some of the most unforgettable attractions at Disney Parks are the parades, which give visitors the chance to see spectacular floats carrying their favorite characters. The parades are always impressive, but the ones that take place during the Holiday season are particularly special. In the Christmas parade at the Tokyo Disney Resort, Mickey Mouse, Minnie Mouse, and Goofy are joined by Duffy the Disney Bear. Duffy was first created in 2002, and since then he has become incredibly popular with Japanese fans of Disney.

THE INSPIRATION
For the Disneyland Paris castle, Imagineers envisioned an imaginative interpretation of the magnificent citadel that is a constant presence of enchantment throughout Walt Disney's *Sleeping Beauty* (1959), as shown in this publicity cel setup.

LE CHÂTEAU DE LA BELLE AU BOIS DORMANT AT DISNEYLAND PARIS
The heavenward-spiraling architecture of Mont St. Michel, the famous French landmark, was a defining influence on Le Château de la Belle au Bois Dormant, which soars 148 ft (45 m) into the sky. The square trees of the movie and the concept art are evident.

STUNNING CONCEPT ART
In this dreamlike concept painting, artist Frank Armitage—who had worked side by side with production designer Eyvind Earle in hand-painting the backgrounds for the original film —reimagined the fairy-tale castle. He incorporated some stylized *Sleeping Beauty* details including Earle's signature square trees in the surrounding landscape.

Castle of Magical Dreams

One of the most distinctive of the Disney theme park castles, Le Château de la Belle au Bois Dormant is also the most fanciful. For this enchanting structure at Disneyland Park in Disneyland Paris, Imagineers sought to build a castle different from any of the many actual fortresses that can be seen in Europe—one that would have more of a fantastical appearance. Through an artful melding of architecture, nature, and fantasy, the designers created a fabulous, dreamlike fort that defies reality. As with all Imagineering projects, it started with a piece of beautiful and inspirational concept art.

A Small Sing-Along

The Disney Parks attraction "it's a small world" allows guests to travel around the world in boats on a gentle musical cruise. Walt asked songwriters Richard M. Sherman and Robert B. Sherman to come up with a simple song that could be repeated over and over, in different languages. The result: one of the most well-known Disney songs of all time. Many regions of the world are represented in the attraction, and there are more than 300 amazing *Audio-Animatronics*® doll-like figures.

SMALL WORLD, BIG DEBUT
Opening on April 22, 1964, "it's a small world" was one of four attractions Walt created for the 1964–65 New York World's Fair, and it quickly became one of the most popular. More than 10 million visitors experienced the musical cruise at the fair.

THE FLAIR OF MARY BLAIR
One of Walt's favorite artists, Mary Blair (right with Walt and left, Imagineer Marc Davis) worked extensively on "it's a small world." The small blonde doll wearing black boots and a poncho seen here is a tribute to Mary and can be spotted halfway up the Eiffel Tower.

BEAUTIFUL COLLAGE
Walt handpicked artist Mary Blair to develop the style and color scheme for the attraction, as seen in this concept art collage. The illustration depicts whimsical interpretations of such European landmarks as the Eiffel Tower, the Leaning Tower of Pisa, and a Dutch windmill.

ALL AROUND THE WORLD
Mary Blair provided concept sketches for environments from all over the world, including this one based on a icy landscape.

DISNEYLAND DEDICATION
When Walt moved "it's a small world" to Disneyland Park in 1966, he dedicated it, accompanied by children, by pouring water that had been gathered from the oceans of the world into the Seven Seaways canal.

THE WORLD OVER
Mary Blair designed the kinetic attraction facade for Disneyland Park. It features an "International Gateway" with stylized spires and whirling, moving finials covered in 22-karat-gold leafing.

WELCOME TO MORE VOICES
The Disneyland attraction welcomed two new singers who use wheelchairs in 2022, one in the Latin American section of the attraction and one in the grand finale. It took more than six months to design and craft the beautiful characters and their wheelchairs.

Welcome, Foolish Mortals

One of the most popular Disney theme park attractions ever, Haunted Mansion has stood on the edge of New Orleans Square in Disneyland Park since 1962–1963, even though the show inside didn't debut for another six years. Originally, it was to be a walk-through attraction, but with Disney's development of the Omnimover transportation system, "Doom Buggies" were invented for guests to ride. It has been home to 999 unearthly specters since opening in 1969—and there's always room for one more. The eerie sights and sounds within Haunted Mansion are presented with a tongue-in-cheek lightheartedness, for as the attraction's Ghost Host himself intones, the Mansion has hot and cold running chills and wall-to-wall creeps.

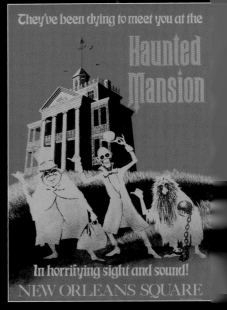

BEWARE
Featuring the Hitchhiking Ghosts, this original 1969 poster by Imagineers Ken Chapman and Marc Davis—one of the attraction's most significant creators—remains at Disneyland Park

DYING FOR A DANCE
One of the most impressive effects in the attraction is the ballroom scene. It features waltzing ghosts that dance around, vanishing and reappearing before guests' eyes!

DEAD EFFECTS
Imagineer Yale Gracey with the notorious Hatbox Ghost. It was removed from the attraction soon after opening due to technical difficulties. With the help of newer technology, the Hatbox Ghost reappeared in May 2015.

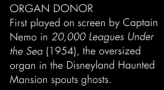

ORGAN DONOR
First played on screen by Captain Nemo in *20,000 Leagues Under the Sea* (1954), the oversized organ in the Disneyland Haunted Mansion spouts ghosts.

MACABRE MUSICIANS
In the Graveyard, spirited specters sing the haunting theme song "Grim Grinning Ghosts."

HOME HAUNTED HOME
Haunted Mansion (seen here with its Haunted Mansion Holiday overlay) is created in the elegant Southern style of its New Orleans Square home. Walt didn't want a traditional decrepit building in Disneyland, saying he'd keep up the outside and let the ghosts take care of the inside.

FESTIVE FRIGHTS
Introduced in 2001, Haunted Mansion Holiday redresses the classic Disneyland Park attraction over the Halloween and Christmas seasons with characters from *Tim Burton's The Nightmare Before Christmas* (1993).

GHOST RIDERS
Haunted Mansion uses the Omnimover ride system. The oval-shaped attraction vehicles move continuously around the Mansion, swiveling to show each guest the sights and the spooks.

Jack Skellington, hero of *Tim Burton's The Nightmare Before Christmas*, greets guests as they enter the ride queue for Haunted Mansion Holiday.

PHANTOM MANOR
Haunted Mansion is known as Phantom Manor at Disneyland Paris. This is Imagineer Bob Baranick with a model of the attraction.

Ahoy, Mateys

The Pirates of the Caribbean attraction was originally envisioned as a walk-through with wax figures, but it soon evolved into a showcase for *Audio-Animatronics*® storytelling. It was one of the most elaborate uses of *Audio-Animatronics*® figures ever attempted by Disney. Walt Disney worked extensively on the attraction, but passed away shortly before its debut in March 1967 at Disneyland. In 2006, it was enhanced with characters from the *Pirates of the Caribbean* films, including Captain Jack Sparrow, which were inspired by the classic attraction. More than 400 Imagineers worked for three years on the research, planning, and installation of these enhancements.

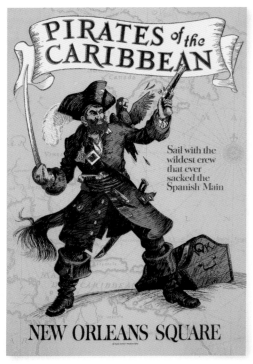

PIRATES of the CARIBBEAN

Sail with the wildest crew that ever sacked the Spanish Main

NEW ORLEANS SQUARE

AVAST, MATEYS!
The pirate on this poster is a self-portrait of Disney artist and Imagineer Collin Campbell, who worked on the design of the original Pirates of the Caribbean attraction.

BURIED BOOTY
Guests travel in boats through scenes of pirate treasure and ghost ships. More than 400,000 gold coins appear in this treasure scene.

MAP TO TREASURE
This concept artwork by Marc Davis is from when the attraction was being developed as a walk-through, and depicts plotting pirates in an atmospheric tavern.

IMITATION OF LIFE
The attraction is populated with 53 *Audio-Animatronics*® animals and birds and 75 *Audio-Animatronics*® pirates and villagers utilizing advanced animatronics technology.

JOLLY ROGER
This concept artwork imagines the first time guests see pirates in action. They must navigate between the pirate ships and dodge cannonballs that land perilously close to their boats.

PIRATE RAID
This evocative study of the "chase scene" is by legendary Imagineer Claude Coats, who was largely responsible for the attraction's intricate settings.

UP IN FLAMES
One of the most elaborate sequences in the attraction is when a pirate raid is foiled and a seaward village is set on fire. As real flames were not an option, the Imagineers developed effects using clever lighting and projection to simulate the blaze.

MUTINY ABOUNDS
Hector Barbossa is a legendary foe to Captain Jack Sparrow on the screen, and he began to haunt park attractions around the globe in 2006. A more ghoulish version appeared in the Paris Disneyland Park in 2017.

Favorite Attractions: Blast Off!

Space Mountain takes voyagers on a thrilling galactic flight past meteorites, stars, and other outer space effects. The indoor roller coaster attraction made its debut in Magic Kingdom Park at Walt Disney World on January 15, 1975. Walt dreamed up the concept in the early 1960s, but it was 11 years before technology caught up with his vision. U.S. astronaut Gordon Cooper joined the creative team as an Imagineering consultant, using information gleaned from NASA's early space missions to make the experience feel like actual space flight.

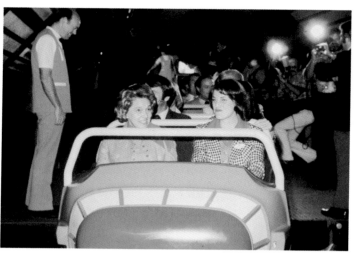

GALACTIC FRONTIER
Disneyland's Space Mountain opened in 1977, two years after its counterpart at Walt Disney World. Guests ride in tandem seat vehicles, rather than the single file vehicles of Walt Disney World's attraction.

FROM THE EARTH TO THE MOON
Imagineers Victoria Aguilera, Pat Doyle, and Tim Stone helped re-imagine the attraction for its debut in Disneyland Paris on June 1, 1995, giving it a Jules Verne-inspired aesthetic.

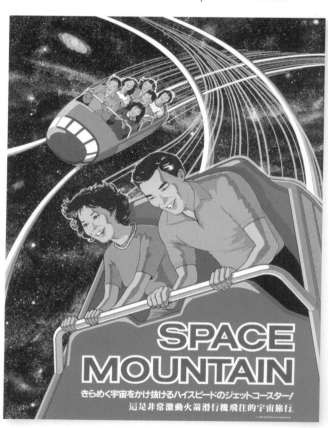

FUTURE ICON
This 1983 poster art emphasizes guests' experience of speed in outer space for the attraction at Tokyo Disneyland. This was the first Space Mountain to debut concurrent with the park's opening.

SPACE MOUNTAIN: MISSION 2
Space Mountain: de la Terre à la Lune in Disneyland Paris underwent a major refurbishment in the early 2000s, and became Space Mountain: Mission 2. Greg Pro and Owen Yoshino designed this poster in 2004 to celebrate the re-launched attraction.

FUTURISTIC MOUNTAIN
Imagineers used concept art like this piece by Christopher Smith, to design the gleaming white, high-tech Tomorrowland "mountain" at Tokyo Disneyland.

UNIVERSALLY THRILLING
The glow of Space Mountain at night attracts guests to experience an out-of-this-world attraction at Tokyo Disneyland.

Bright Lights

Disney Parks shine after dark with spectacular magic and special effects.

▲ For over a half century, the *Main Street Electrical Parade* has lit up the eyes and hearts of Disneyland and other Disney Park visitors.

A whole new phase of fun kicks off once the sun goes down in Disney Parks. From LED-lit parades and vibrant stage shows to sky-high pyrotechnics, the evening hours are full of glowing entertainment.

ON THE STREET

Main Street Electrical Parade first lit up Disneyland in California in 1972, with a continuous run through 1996. Featuring floats, live entertainers, and over 600,000 LED lights in the current rendition, the popular parade has since reappeared in limited engagements in its original space, as well as at Disney California Adventure. Alternative versions have lit up all other Disney Parks around the globe: through the years, these parades have been titled *SpectroMagic*, *Fantillusion*, *Light Magic*, *Tokyo Disneyland Electrical Parade Dreamlights*, *Paint the Night Parade*, and *Disney's Electric Parade*.

▲ The *Electrical Water Pageant* is aglow and afloat at the Seven Seas Lagoon in Disney's Polynesian Villas & Bungalows.

▼ All eyes are on festivities celebrating Mickey's Halloween Party at Disneyland.

SPECTACULAR SPECTACLES

Fantasmic! debuted in 1992 at Disneyland, a multisensory show portraying the imagination of Mickey Mouse that includes characters, music, lasers, water effects, pyrotechnics, mist screen projections, and more magical elements playing against a naturally dark backdrop. Disney's Hollywood Studios and Tokyo DisneySea have also hosted the show. Tokyo DisneySea has presented a number of glowing spectacles, including *DisneySea Symphony*, *BraviSEAmo*, and *Disney Light the Night*, all of which choreographed glorious fireworks displays with favorite Disney

music. Florida resorts have hosted *Fantasmic!* as well as shows called *Disney Enchantment, Harmonious, Electrical Water Pageant, Tree of Life Awakenings,* and *Wonderful World of Animation,* while Disneyland Paris has offered *Disney D-Light* using drone technology.

OVER THE CASTLE

The magical display of fireworks over Disney Parks castles has become an iconic visual feast: so striking that it has long been part of the banner title card used by various films from The Walt Disney Studios. This tradition makes hearts and eyes flutter, with the majesty of light and sound as a beautiful endcap to a magical day spent at the happiest places on earth.

▲ 240 culturally diverse performers brought Disney stories and people from all around the world together in EPCOT's *Harmonious,* part of the Walt Disney World 50th Anniversary celebrations.

▼ A spectacular display of fireworks and projection technology illuminate Cinderella Castle in *Happily Ever After* at Magic Kingdom Park.

Magic By Land and By Sea

Extending Disney fun beyond theme parks and into Disney-hosted accommodations adds a whole other level to the vacation experience.

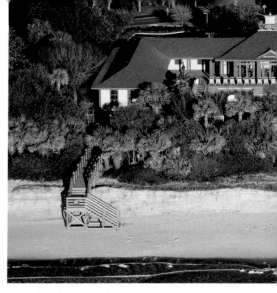

▲ The Beach House, above, is a quick shuttle ride away from the main area of Disney's Hilton Head Island Resort.

The concept of Disney guests being hosted overnight reaches all the way back to the launch of theme parks, when Walt realized that driving to (then-remote) Anaheim to visit Disneyland might be best complemented with a stay in a local hotel. He convinced his friend Jack Wrather to build and run a "motor inn" on Disney property near the theme park, and thus arose the Disneyland Hotel, which opened in 1955. The hotel was owned by the Wrather Corporation until The Walt Disney Company acquired the business in 1988, and since then, it has undergone a number of expansions and upgrades to become central to what is now known as the Disneyland Resort.

▲ The Disneyland Hotel is connected directly to Disneyland via a Monorail station that was added in 1961. Two Monorail-themed slides snake around the hotel's pool.

◄ Aulani, A Disney Resort & Spa, is located in Ko 'Olina, O'ahu, Hawai'i. The resort celebrates the legends and traditions of Hawaiian culture through music, art, and storytelling.

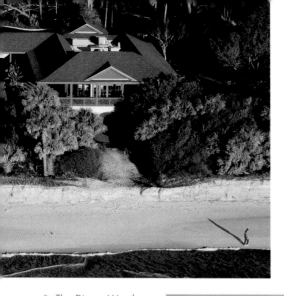

RIDE-FREE RESORTS

Some regions of the United States host amazing Disney vacation experiences without a nearby Disney theme park. These locations focus on the natural beauty and unique recreational options of each region, and each resort opens its doors with the warm family welcome that The Walt Disney Company has long practiced. Disney's Vero Beach Resort opened on Florida's Atlantic Treasure Coast in 1995. With design inspired by 1940s-era Carolina Lowcountry vacation lodges, Disney's Hilton Head Island Resort opened on the coast of South Carolina in 1996. Aulani, A Disney Resort & Spa opened in 2011 in Hawai'i on the southwest coastline of O'ahu, and is known to host Mickey Mouse and other character friends in vacation wear.

▶ The *Disney Wonder* and other Disney cruise ships have a specially crafted ship's horn that plays the opening seven-note theme of "When You Wish Upon a Star" from *Pinocchio* (1940).

FLOATING FUN

Disney Cruise Line was the first company in its industry to commission ships especially designed to host family accommodations. As of 2023, five Disney ships explore a wide range of ocean destinations, with the *Disney Magic* being launched in 1998, *Disney Wonder* in 1999, *Disney Dream* in 2011, *Disney Fantasy* in 2012, and *Disney Wish* in 2022. One of the most unique ports visited by Disney Cruise Line is Castaway Cay, a private island in The Bahamas. Formerly known as Gorda Cay, Disney created a magical retreat at this island location over the course of 18 months.

▲ Castaway Cay offers a beautiful place to anchor the *Disney Dream*. It features a beach-based environment for Mickey Mouse and friends, as well as cruising guests.

Fan-tasyland

While there have been devotees of all things Disney for over a century, an official fan club for them to share the joy is a relatively new and exciting concept.

▲ The efforts of original company archivist and Disney Legend Dave Smith continue through an amazing staff and the leadership of Rebecca Cline, seen here.

Launched in 2009, D23 ("D" for Disney and "23" in honor of the year 1923, when Walt arrived in California and founded the namesake company) has centralized the passion and energy of Disney fans. This official fan club offers them access to special events, advance screenings, breaking news, and exclusive mementos from all aspects of the company's creative wells.

EVERYTHING OLD IS NEW AGAIN

Part of what makes D23 special is the depth of history it celebrates—lovingly curated with the help of the Walt Disney Archives. In this magical place, historical objects are preserved and shared with later generations, and

landmark anniversaries are recognized. The Archives even have their own Disney+ documentary, *Adventure Thru the Walt Disney Archives*, hosted by Disney Legend Don Hahn.

EXCITING EVENTS

D23 brings Disney fun to different cities for fans to enjoy in various corners of the world. Members might be invited to attend a live theater performance of *The Lion King*, and then listen to cast members talk about their experiences after the show on Broadway in New York City; they might get into the holiday spirit with a 30th anniversary screening of

The Muppet Christmas Carol at Walt Disney World near Orlando, Florida, complete with Christmas cookie treats and an Ugly Sweater Contest; or they might attend a full-scale convention like D23 Expo. The Expo was the original event launching the D23 wave of excitement, and since its four-day initial presence in Anaheim, California in 2009, has included presentations on Disney history, celebrity appearances, a fan costume contest, and first looks at upcoming film, video game, and attraction updates. It also features pop-up shops with exclusive merchandise, curated exhibits, memorabilia trading centers, and the Disney Legends Awards Ceremony.

◄ A curated display case by the Walt Disney Archives, featured at D23 Expo Japan 2018.

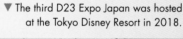

▼ The third D23 Expo Japan was hosted at the Tokyo Disney Resort in 2018.

In June 2019, D23 guests celebrated the 40th anniversary of the *Mickey Mouse Disco* album with a Throwback Thursday night of roller skating in Glendale, California. They were also treated to a skate performance by Mickey and Minnie Mouse in their groovy 1970s regalia.

Disney100: The Exhibition is a special traveling event celebrating the century mark of The Walt Disney Company, and D23 guests were invited to attend a special breakfast gathering and the opening ceremony in Philadelphia in February 2023.

MEMBER MEMORABILIA

Disney fans are often avid collectors of fun memorabilia, from character-themed items to location-specific souvenirs. While Mickey Mouse watches and Mickey Mouse Ear Hats are perhaps the most well-recognized legacy collectibles, some of the more popular recent items include trading pins and Funko Pop! figurines, with thousands of options to choose and trade.

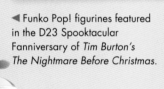

Funko Pop! figurines featured in the D23 Spooktacular Fanniversary of *Tim Burton's The Nightmare Before Christmas.*

A cross-over D23 Fanniversary collection of buttons celebrates *Hocus Pocus* and *Tim Burton's The Nightmare Before Christmas.*

HONORING THE GREATS

Since 1987, The Walt Disney Company has recognized individuals who have deeply contributed to its rich history by naming them Disney Legends. Honorees are memorialized through bronze plaques that may feature handprints and signatures, housed in Legends Plaza near the Team Disney Building in Burbank, California. In 2009, D23 Expo began hosting the honoree ceremony as part of their biannual gatherings.

Roy E. Disney at the 2006 Disney Legends Ceremony

▲ In *Kingdom Hearts III*, Goofy, Sora, and Donald Duck face the evil Heartless forces, who want to spread their darkness over the entire universe.

Virtual Playtime

Video games allow Disney fans to experience their favorite worlds and characters in epic new ways.

▲ Tinker Bell, Mike Wazowski, Merida, and Stitch come together in Toy Box mode for unique adventures in *Disney Infinity*.

▶ In *Disney Tsum Tsum*, players restack the toys that have fallen from shelves in a Disney Store.

In the 1980s, Disney sparked its first internal development and publishing of computer and video games. Some of the first titles were Disney Software programs that enabled fans to customize their own Mouse-emblazoned greeting cards in *Mickey & Minnie's Fun Time Print Kit*, or learn how to read with the help of favorite characters in *Follow the Reader*. Since then, Disney games have evolved over the decades on the latest technological platforms. From desktop computer software and gaming consoles to multi-platform systems and arcade machines, characters continue to soar into new entertainment experiences with original stories and unique art styles.

SORA AND FRIENDS

Sora is determined to save his homeland from the evil Heartless villains, and travels through a number of notable Disney worlds such as Timeless River and Beast's Castle in various releases of the *Kingdom Hearts* games series. The series launched in 2002 and tells an original story that weaves an epic tale featuring some of Disney's most iconic characters such as Donald Duck and Goofy.

A BOTTOMLESS TOY BOX

Video games were taken to a whole new level with the launch of *Disney Infinity* in 2013. Fans and gamers are immersed in an action-adventure storytelling world where toy versions of characters from different Disney and Pixar worlds coexist—Mr. Incredible can ride Cinderella's coach, or Merida can board Captain Jack Sparrow's ship. In Play Set mode, the gameplay is themed to a single story, while in Toy Box mode, players can create their own journey and tell unique stories using myriad characters and without any rules.

MULTIDIMENSIONAL FUN

Disney Tsum Tsum (tsum being a term inspired by the Japanese verb "tsumu" meaning "to stack") launched

▲ Riddle Rosehearts serves as the Housewarden of Heartslabyul in *Disney Twisted Wonderland*.

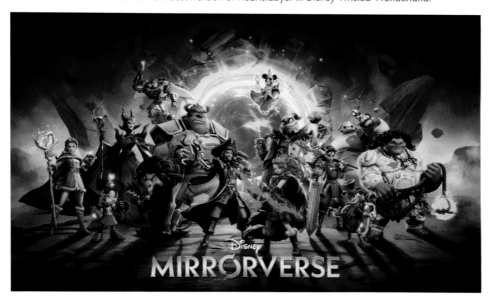

▲ Maui, Minnie Mouse, and other Guardians are battle-ready in *Disney Mirrorverse*.

▲ Mickey Mouse and friends jump, climb, swim, and take action in a number of other fun animated ways in *Disney Illusion Island*.

in Japan in 2013 through arcade and mobile puzzle game experiences, challenging players to stack toys. Tsum Tsum fun later found its way into the real world as popular stackable plush versions of Disney characters, and also expanded into the console gaming world via *Disney Tsum Tsum Festival* in 2019.

EDUCATING THE EVIL-DOERS

When players enter the world of *Disney Twisted Wonderland*, they are teleported to Night Raven College, a school inspired by Disney villains. Experiencing the lessons, stories, and tests of university life, players encounter characters housed in various dorms inspired by classic Disney villains, such as Heartslabyul based on the Queen of Hearts and her cards, or Savanaclaw based on Scar. Launched in 2020, *Twisted Wonderland* has conjured such a large fan base that manga and novel versions have appeared as well.

ALTERNATE REALITY

In *Disney Mirrorverse*, numerous evolved Disney and Pixar characters from Aladdin to Zurg become powerful Guardians in a divergent reality. Released in 2022, this mobile game invites players to assemble teams of Guardians to defend the Mirrorverse and its worlds—reflections of familiar Pixar and Disney worlds that have been amplified by magic—against a treacherous threat.

BOOKS TO THE RESCUE

In the 2023 *Disney Illusion Island* game, players can choose the role of hand-drawn Mickey or one of his classic cartoon friends as they save the mysterious island of Monoth and its furry inhabitants by recovering three stolen mystical books. Players can play with up to three others in this illustrated adventure.

"...curiosity keeps leading us down new paths." WALT DISNEY

All Things Disney

Mickey Mouse Memorabilia

By 1929, Mickey Mouse was a bona fide box-office star, and his public wanted much more. While it may have seemed only logical to let everyone have their favorite Mickey Mouse in their very own house, the Mickey merchandise boom actually started with a chance encounter in a New York hotel lobby. A man asked Walt Disney for permission to produce a Mickey children's writing tablet and the excitement for Mickey memorabilia was born. Since that day, his ear-to-ear smile has appeared on an infinite number of primo products, including umbrellas, soap, and wallpaper.

1 Folding chair, Crawford Furniture Mfg. Co. (1934) **2** Belt buckle display, Cervantes, Limited Edition (1976)
3 Coming Home game, Marks Brothers (1930s) **4** Christmas lights, Noma Electric Corp. (1930s) **5** Candlestick phone, N. N. Hill Brass Co. (1930s)
6 Tin watering can, Ohio Art Co. (1930s) **7** Big Little Books, Whitman Publishing Co. (1930s) **8** Gum Ball Vending Bank, Hasbro (1970s)
9 Fun-E-Flex Mickey, Nifty/Flex-E-Flex Toys for George Borgfeldt Corp. (1930s) **10** Handcar, Lionel Corporation (1930s)
11 Mickey Math Calculator, Omron for Alco. (1975) **12** Trapeze, George Borgfeldt Corp. (1930s) **13** Mousegetar Jr., Marx (1960s)
14 Hankies display standee, Hermann Handkerchief Co., Inc. (1930s) **15** Tie bar, D.H. Neumann Co. (1930s) **16** Watch, Ingersoll-Waterbury Co. (1930s)
17 Old Maid card game, Whitman Publishing Co. (1930s) **18** Mickey the Musician, Louis Marx & Co. Inc. (1960s)
19 Tea tray, Ohio Art Co. (1930s) **20** Mickey Mouse Club phonograph (c.1950s) **21** Telephone, American Telecommunications Corp. (1977)
22 Party horns, Marks Brothers Co. of Boston (1930s) **23** Cowboy Mickey Mouse doll, Knickerbocker Toy Co. (1936)
24 Art Deco radio, Emerson Radio and Phonograph Corp. (1934)

Disneyland Collectibles

When the gates of Disneyland Park first opened in 1955, Walt Disney wanted to ensure guests were able to take home a piece of magic so they could relive their experience. From traditional mementoes such as hats to more novel keepsakes including dolls and charms, Disneyland souvenirs were all designed with that distinctive Disney touch. Early memorabilia that has been lovingly preserved is particularly coveted by Disney collectors. Here from the Walt Disney Archives is a treasure trove of perfectly preserved artifacts from Disneyland Park.

1

2

3

4

5

6

7

8

9

10

11

12

1 Press preview day ticket (July 17, 1955) 2 Ticket No.1, purchased by Roy O. Disney (July 18, 1955)
3 "Mickey Mouse Club Circus" admission ticket (1955) 4 *The Story of Disneyland* guidebook [front cover] (1955)
5 *The Story of Disneyland* guidebook [back cover] (1955) 6 Mickey Mouse pencil sharpener (1955) 7 "Little Law Man" sheriff badge
8 Miniature camera viewer (1950s) 9 Tinker Bell's Magic Wand, Glow in the Dark (1950s) 10 Keppy Kap (1950s)
11 Space Specs "Sun Glare Protection" 12 Eraser Set (1960s) 13 Pirates of the Caribbean cuff links & tie clip (1960s)
14 Ticket Book [Front Cover] (1950s/1960s) 15 Ticket Book [B, C, D, E tickets] (1950s/1960s) 16 Disneyland tattoos (1950s)
17 Felt pennant 18 Matterhorn bobsleds key chain (1960s) 19 "Mickey Mouse" Disneyland bolo tie 20 Tour Guide doll (1960s)
21 Fantasyland View-Master® stereo pictures (1960s) 22 The Primeval World, "Dimetrodon" figurine (1964)
23 "Floaty" Fountain Pens: Monorail (top, green) and Submarine Voyage (bottom, red) 24 Charm Bracelet (1950s)

A Very Rare Toy

Donald Duck was all the rage (apt considering the Duck's explosive temper) from the moment he first waddled onto the silver screen in 1934. By 1935, as a testament to Donald's overnight stardom, Donald Duck soap, ties, handkerchiefs, and other memorabilia filled shop shelves. At first, Donald had a long thin neck and an extended, narrow beak. This early style continued for only a year or two, making the dolls, toys, and other "long-billed" memorabilia manufactured from 1934 to 1936 eagerly sought-after collector's items. The ducky products from this period often featured one of the quarrelsome quackster's eyes closed in a wink, indicating Donald's mischievous nature.

ORIGINAL MODEL SHEET
This original model sheet from 1934 was created by character designer Ferdinand Horvath for Donald's first appearance in *The Wise Little Hen* (1934). The style was maintained through 1936 until the character was re-designed with the cuter appearance we know today.

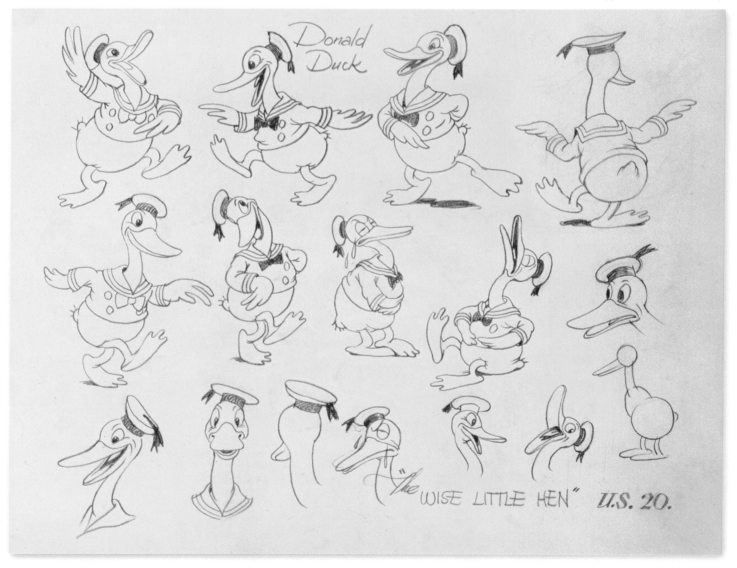

LONG-BILLED DONALD
This vintage toy is one of many "long-billed" Duck toys made from 1934 through 1936. It was made in Japan for distribution in the United States.

The signature long bill indicates that this is memorabilia from Donald's earliest era.

The long neck is another indication of this sought-after era of Donald merchandise.

The Disney artists gave Donald a sailor suit because they saw him as a rascally little boy—and because Walt pointed out that ducks like water!

Paint captures the red tie and blue blouse of Donald's trademark sailor suit.

Though not visible here, Donald's fingers were originally intended to be feathers, but soon evolved into actual digits.

During this early period, Donald's famous webbed feet were fuller and more pronounced. They were later redesigned to be flatter.

Making a Point

Disney collectors have sought out Disney pins since the 1930s, but it was in 1999 that Disney Pin Trading became a phenomenon, as Disney Parks began a new tradition of official pin trading with the kickoff of the Millennium Celebration at Walt Disney World Resort. Designed by Disney artists, each individual cloisonné, semi-cloisonné, and hard-enamel metal pin undergoes a painstaking processes of hand assembly, molding, painting, polishing, and firing to create a shining emblem of Disneyana. Pin traders, also called "pin pals," can collect thousands and thousands of individual designs commemorating characters, attractions, films, television, and special events.

1 Olaf: Disney Parks, 2014 2 Tokyo Disney Resort 30th Anniversary 3 Ludwig Von Drake 40th Anniversary: Walt Disney World Resort, 2001
4 Commuter Assistance: The Walt Disney Studios, 1998 5 Walt Disney Animation Studios 90th Anniversary, 2013
6 Disneyland Mouseorail: Disney Decade Pin: Disneyland Resort, 1990 7 Walk in Walt's Footsteps Tour: Disneyland Resort, 1990
8 Disney Cruise Line: 2nd anniversary of ship launch, 2002 9 Star Tours Design/Construction Team,1994 10 Mariachi Minnie: Disneyland Resort, 2001
11 Pop Century Resort: *Mickey's PhilharMagic Mission: Space* opening, 2003 12 *The Hunchback of Notre Dame*: Limited edition, 2014 13 Tigger: Disney Parks, 2014
14 Gateway to Dreams: Disneyland Resort, 2005 15 Epcot: Spaceship Earth: Walt Disney World Resort, 2005 16 Oswald the Lucky Rabbit: Disney Parks, 2013
17 "it's a small world": Blast to the Past: A Celebration of Walt Disney Art Classics, 2004 18 Evil Queen: Villains pin series: Disneyland Resort, 1991
19 1955 Cast member replica badge: Disneyland Resort, 2004 20 Celebrate Mickey 75 Years of Fun: The Walt Disney Studios, 2003
21 Peter Pig: Surprise Pin Series: Disney Parks, 2014 22 Disney Legends induction ceremony, D23 Expo, 2009 23 Walt's Legacy Collection: Walt Disney Resort, 2005
24 Euro Disney Opening Cast Member Pin: Frontierland, 1992 25 Chandu: Tokyo DisneySea, 2013 26 Snow White: Given out at Radio City Music Hall in New York, 1987
27 Mickey Mouse Jack O' Lantern, 28 Club 33: 33rd anniversary celebration, Disneyland Resort, 2000 29 Duffy the Disney Bear: Aulani (Disney resort & spa), 2014
30 Disneyana shop: Disneyland Resort, 1992 31 Mickey Mouse Weekly, England, Mickey Mouse Chums, 1936
32 Disney's California Adventure: The Twilight Zone Tower of Terror™: Rose Parade Limited Edition, 2004 33 Euro Disney opening crew: Cast member exclusive, 1992
34 Sorcerer Mickey: The Walt Disney Company Canadian release, 1989 35 The Walt Disney Company Annual Report, Disneyland 50th Anniversary Cast Member Gift, 2005
36 Happy Birthday Donald Duck: Disney Channel: Giveaway at NTCA Trade Convention, Las Vegas, 1984 37 Chicken Little: Pin Trading University: Walt Disney Resort, 2008
38 Big Bad Wolf: Villains Pin Series: Disneyland Resort, 1991 39 Donald Duck: Stitch's High Sea Adventure, Scavenger Hunt: Disney Cruise Line, 2005
40 Fantasyland: Disneyland Resort Give Giver Extraordinaire, 1986 41 Mickey Mouse Health Brigade, c.1934

Index

Credits

TIM BURTON'S THE NIGHTMARE BEFORE
CHRISTMAS (1993)
The movie, *Tim Burton's The Nightmare Before
Christmas*, story and characters by Tim Burton.
Copyright © 1993 Disney Enterprises, Inc.

FRANKENWEENIE (2012)
Copyright © 2012 Disney Enterprises, Inc.

WINNIE THE POOH characters are based on
the "Winnie-the-Pooh" works, by A. A. Milne
and E. H. Shepard.

ONE HUNDRED AND ONE DALMATIANS
Based on the book The Hundred and One
Dalmatians by Dodie Smith, published by
The Viking Press.

THE ARISTOCATS is based on the book by
Thomas Rowe.

THE RESCUERS AND THE RESCUERS DOWN
UNDER feature characters from the Disney film
suggested by the books by Margery Sharp,
The Rescuers and Miss Bianca, published by
Little, Brown and Company.

The movie THE PRINCESS AND THE FROG
Copyright © 2009 Disney, story inspired in part
by the book THE FROG PRINCESS by E.D. Baker
Copyright © 2002, published by Bloomsbury
Publishing, Inc.

THE LION KING (1994)
Song: "Hakuna Matata"
© 1994 Wonderland Music Company, Inc.

MARY POPPINS (1964)
The Disney movie, *Mary Poppins* is based
on the Mary Poppins stories by P.L. Travers.

PIRATES OF THE CARIBBEAN
© Disney Enterprises, Inc.
Curse of the Black Pearl: (2003)
Based on the screenplay by Ted Elliot and
Terry Rossio and Jay Wolpert
Produced by Jerry Bruckheimer
Directed by Gore Verbinski

DEAD MAN'S CHEST (2006)
Based on the screenplay by Ted Elliot
& Terry Rossio
Based on the characters created by Ted Elliot &
Terry Rossio and Stuart Beattie and Jay Wolpert
Based on Walt Disney's Pirates of the Caribbean
Produced by Jerry Bruckheimer
Directed by Gore Verbinski

AT WORLD'S END (2007)
Based on the screenplay by Ted Elliot
& Terry Rossio
Based on the characters created by Ted Elliot
& Terry Rossio and Stuart Beattie and Jay Wolpert
Based on Walt Disney's Pirates of the Caribbean
Produced by Jerry Bruckheimer
Directed by Gore Verbinski

ON STRANGER TIDES (2011)
Based on characters created by Ted Elliott
& Terry Rossio and Stuart Beattie and Jay Wolpert
Based on Walt Disney's Pirates of the Caribbean
Suggested by the novel by Tim Powers
Screen Story and Screenplay
by Ted Elliott & Terry Rossio

HANNAH MONTANA (TV SERIES)
Based on the series created by Michael Poryes
and Rich Correll & Barry O'Brien

HIGH SCHOOL MUSICAL 1, 2
Based on the Disney Channel original movie
"High School Musical," written by Peter Barsocchini

Walt Disney World® Resort
Disneyland® Resort
Disneyland® Park
Disney California Adventure® Park
Disneyland® Paris
Tokyo Disney Resort®
Tokyo Disneyland® Park
Tokyo DisneySea® Park
Magic Kingdom®
Main Street, U.S.A.®
Adventureland®
Frontierland®
Fantasyland®
Tomorrowland®
Epcot® Theme Park
Disney's Animal Kingdom® Theme Park

THE GREAT MOUSE DETECTIVE (1986)
Based on the 'Basil of Baker Street' book series
by Eve Titus and Paul Galdone.

Slinky ® Dog © Just Play LLC

Photo Credits

All images © Disney

p.145 tl Photo by Deborah Coleman / Pixar;
p.145 bl Photo by Deborah Coleman / Pixar;

All art images not specifically credited to a named
artist are attributed to Disney Studio Artist.

Sources

p.63: "Animals have personalities … " https://
d23.com/walts-quotes-category/nature/
p.89: "He has a power … " *The Art of Hercules:
The Chaos of Creation* by Stephen Rebello and
Jane Healey, p.101
p.99: "Not only was … " *The Art of Meet the
Robinsons* by Tracey Miller-Zarneke, p.58
p.109: "The music is …" *Frozen 2* press kit, p.18
p.113: "Even in an early … " *The Art of Zootopia*
by Jessica Julius, p.31
p.114: "the ocean connects … " *The Art of Moana*
by Jessica Julius and Maggie Malone, p.70
p.115: "This connection to … " ibid. p.13
p.116: "… it's so rare that … " *Raya and The Last
Dragon* Press Conference, 2021
p.119: "It's an imagined …" *The Art of Strange
World* by Juan Pablo Reyes Lancaster Jones and
Kalikolehua Hurley, p.16
p.148: "We always knew …" Jason Katz, *The Art
of Coco*, p.158
p.149: "Almost any moment … " *Soul* press kit, p.2
p.150: "It's a love letter … " *Luca* press kit, p.1
p.151: "We're all imperfect … " *Turning Red* press
kit, p.6
p.187: "The yearning of …" *Pinocchio* press kit, p.4
p.191: "This is a musical …" *Aladdin* press kit, p.11
p.242: "…curiosity keeps leading … " https://
d23.com/walts-quotes-category/technology/

Senior Editor Ruth Amos
Senior Designers Lisa Robb, Clive Savage
Cover Design Mark Penfound
Production Editor Marc Staples
Senior Production Controller Mary Slater
Managing Editor Emma Grange
Managing Art Editor Vicky Short
Publishing Director Mark Searle

This edition published in 2023
First published in Great Britain in 2015 by
Dorling Kindersley Limited
DK, One Embassy Gardens, 8 Viaduct Gardens,
London SW11 7BW

The authorised representative in the EEA is
Dorling Kindersley Verlag GmbH. Arnulfstr. 124,
80636 Munich, Germany

Page design copyright © 2023 Dorling Kindersley Limited
A Penguin Random House Company

10 9 8 7 6 5 4 3 2 1
001–332207–Oct/2023

A CIP catalogue record for this book
is available from the British Library.
ISBN: 978-0-2415-7368-6

Printed and bound in China

For the curious
www.dk.com

MIX
Paper | Supporting
responsible forestry
FSC™ C018179

This book was made with Forest
Stewardship Council™ certified
paper – one small step in DK's
commitment to a sustainable future.
For more information, go to
www.dk.com/our-green-pledge.

ACKNOWLEDGEMENTS

DK would like to thank Tracey Miller-Zarneke for her authorial expertise and enthusiasm; Jim Fanning and Barbara Bazaldua for their text in the original edition; Chelsea Alon, Kellee Hartman, Fox Carney, Doug Engalla, Ann Hansen, Jackie Vasquez, Rebecca Cline, Joanna Pratt, Michael Buckhoff, Kevin M. Kern, Hope Mackenzie, Dale Kennedy, Emily Shartle, Danielle Song, Erin Glover, Elise Aliberti, Kyle Zabala, Matthew Bergeron, Christopher Painter, Jackson Kaplan, Alison Giordano, Jennifer Spring, Chuck Wilson, Nicole Spiegel, Wendy Lefkon, Elizabeth Ansfield, Carlotta Quattrocolo, Heather Knowles, Emily Budin, Patricia Van Note, Joe Sullivan, Miriam Ogawa, Gregory Lee, and Holly Rice at Disney; Jay Ward at Pixar Animation Studios; Sadie Doherty and Brandi Pomfret at Tim Burton Productions; Kate Sayer and Marta Bescos for picture research assistance; Victoria Taylor for proofreading; Matt Jones for editorial assistance; Grace Wynter at Tessera Editorial; Raven Kameʻenui-Becker, Omar Ramadan-Santiago, Antara Dutt, Dee Hudson, Johanie Martinez-Cools, and Vida Cruz-Borja for sensitivity reading; and Vanessa Bird for indexing.

The publisher would also like to thank the following people for their work on the original edition: Chelsea Alon, Justin Arthur, Amy Astley, Simon Beecroft, Alex Bell, Holly Brobst, Michael Buckhoff, Fox Carney, Jo Casey, Sumedha Chopra, Rebecca Cline, Debby Coleman, Kristie Crawford, Beth Davies, Stephanie Everett, David Fentiman, Julie Ferris, Christine Freeman, Mik Gates, Amanda Ghobadi, Ann Hansen, Michael Jusko, Sol Kawage, Dale Kennedy, Kevin M. Kern, Lisa Lanzarini, Wendy Lefkon, Julia March, Myriam Megharbi, Betsy Mercer, Lynne Moulding, Jennifer Murray, Lauren Nesworthy, Alissa Newton, Obinna Ogbunamiri, Beatrice Osman, Edward Ovalle, Scott Piehl, Anna Pond, Joanna Pratt, Frank Reifsnyder, Alesha Reyes, Mark Richards, Sam Richiardi, Lisa Robb, Anna Sander, Diane Scoglio, Anne Sharples, Rima Simonian, Dave Smith, Sadie Smith, Ron Stobbart, Victoria Taylor, Shiho Tilley, Jackie Vasquez, and Mary Walsh.